RUSSIAN CRITICS ON THE CINEMA OF GLASNOST

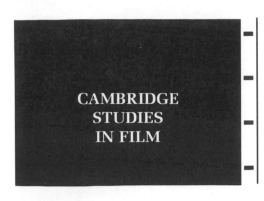

## CAMBRIDGE STUDIES IN FILM

GENERAL EDITORS

Henry Breitrose, *Stanford University*
William Rothman, *University of Miami*

ADVISORY BOARD

Dudley Andrew, *University of Iowa*
Anthony Smith, *Magdalen College, Oxford*
Colin Young, *National Film School*

RECENT TITLES IN THE SERIES

*Nonindifferent Nature: Film and the Structure of Things*, by Sergei Eisenstein (trans. Herbert Marshall)
*Constructivism in Film: The Man with the Movie Camera*, by Vlada Petric
*Inside Soviet Film Satire: Laughter with a Lash*, by Andrew Horton, ed.
*Melodrama and Asian Cinema*, by Wimal Dissanayake
*Film at the Intersection of High and Mass Culture*, by Paul Coates
*Another Frank Capra*, by Leland Poague

# RUSSIAN CRITICS ON THE CINEMA OF GLASNOST

*Edited by*

MICHAEL BRASHINSKY
*The School of Visual Arts,*
*The New School, Brooklyn College of*
*the City University of New York*

ANDREW HORTON
*Loyola University*

CAMBRIDGE
UNIVERSITY PRESS

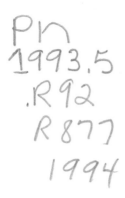

Published by the Press Syndicate of the University of Cambridge
The Pitt Building, Trumpington Street, Cambridge CB2 1RP
40 West 20th Street, New York, NY 10011–4211, USA
10 Stamford Road, Oakleigh, Melbourne 3166, Australia

First published 1994

Printed in the United States of America

*Library of Congress Cataloging-in-Publication Data*
Russian critics on the cinema of glasnost / edited by Michael
    Brashinsky, Andrew Horton.
        p.      cm. – (Cambridge studies in film)
    Articles translated from Russian.
    Filmography: p.
    Includes index.
    ISBN 0-521-44475-6
    1. Motion pictures – Russian S.F.S.R. – reviews.   2. Motion
pictures – Political aspects – Russian S.F.S.R.   I. Brashinsky,
Michael, 1965-      .   II. Horton, Andrew.   III. Series.
PN1993.5.R92R877      1994
791.43'75'0947–dc20                                   93-43590
                                                           CIP

A catalog record for this book is available from the British Library

ISBN 0-521-44475-6 hardback

# Contents

# Acknowledgments

A number of individuals offered helpful suggestions regarding the selection of articles for this anthology. We want to extend our gratitude to Russian critics Sergei Dobrotvorsky, Maya Turovskaya, and Alexander Timofeevsky.

We are also grateful to the translators Mikhail Khazin, Ekaterina Dobrotvorskaya, Margo Mallar, Svetlana Ustinova, and Steve McCormick, who made it possible for this book to appear in English.

Marina Drozdova, Tatyana Mushtakova, Irina Popova, Alexander Kiselev, and Pyotr Shepotinnik of various Moscow publications provided us with considerable assistance in the preparation of the introductory material. We are profoundly thankful.

In the United States:

Our deep appreciation to Nancy Ramsey, who helped inestimably in the final stages of preparing the manuscript, and to Eileen Lottman, who supported this project from its first to its final steps.

Margo Mallar, Stephanie J. Prowant, and Dawn DeFalco helped in the various stages of assembling the manuscript.

Special thanks to the following sources for permission to reprint articles:

*Cinema Without Cinema*, from *Iskusstvo kino*, 1988, No. 6; *The World As a Mirror For the Other World*, from *Kino i zritel*, Vol 2., Moscow, 1988, © Kinocenter, reprinted by permission of Mikhail Yampolsky.

*The Last Romantics*, from *Iskusstvo kino*, 1989, No. 5; *Scherzo–Suite–Nocturne*, from *Iskusstvo kino*, 1988, No. 3; *The Tenderest Shroud*, from *Iskusstvo kino*, 1988, No. 8; reprinted by permission of Alexander Timofeevsky.

*Cinema for Every Day*, from *Literaturnaya gazeta*, 1989, July 14, No. 24, reprinted by permission of Yuri Bogomolov.

*On the Road That Leads to the Truth*, from *Repentance*. Moscow: Kinocenter, 1988; reprinted by permission of Tatyana Khloplyankina. Originally published in *Moskovskaya pravda*, 1987, February 4.

*Between the Circus and the Zoo*, from *Cine Phantom*, 1987, No. 7/8, reprinted by permission of Igor Aleinikov and *Cine Phantom*.

*Is It Easy To Be Grown Up?*, from *Kino*, Riga, 1987, No. 7; reprinted by permission of Lev Anninsky.

*Commissar*, from *Soviet Film*, 1988, No. 5; *Days of Eclipse*, from *Sovetskaya kul'tura*, 1989, Jan. 31, reprinted by permission of Maya Turovskaya.

*Forward, Singing*, from *Leningradskii rabochii*, weekly, 1988, Sept. 16; *A Billion Years Before the End of Cinema*, from *Iskusstvo kino*, 1988, No. 12, reprinted by permission of Tatyana Moskvina.

*Out of Bounds*, from *Sovetskaya kul'tura*, 1989, Jan. 31, reprinted by permission of Victor Bozhovich.

*A Dandy of the Post-Punk Era*, from *Iskusstvo kino*, 1989, No. 3, reprinted by permission of Marina Drozdova.

Several articles were written especially for this collection.

The articles, previously published in Russian, have appeared originally in a slightly different form.

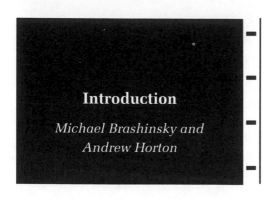

# Introduction

*Michael Brashinsky and*
*Andrew Horton*

In 1978, long before this anthology (or, for that matter, *glasnost* itself) was conceived, a book titled *America on the Screen* appeared briefly on the Moscow bookstands. Published during the cultural vacuum of Brezhnev's stagnation, that book – a collection of American film reviews from the 1970s, reprinted (who knows if legally) from every major U.S. publication – was unprecedented and extraordinary. The movies critiqued in the book, *The Godfather, Cabaret, M.A.S.H., The Exorcist, Scarecrow,* and *Catch-22,* among others, had never been seen (some were never even heard of) by Soviet audiences. Remarkably, it was not the films nor the film makers but the critics – Andrew Sarris, Richard Schickel, Rex Reed, and others – who became heralds of the American screen and, more remarkably, of the American culture and America itself to people who were not allowed to know. If Pauline Kael was feared on the Hudson, she was indeed trusted on the Moscow River.

Since then, the world has turned 180 degrees. Pauline Kael has retired. The USSR is no more. The country, its communist regime, its unelected leaders, and its old names have all ceased to exist. Yet one of the few things that remains unchanged is the unenlightenment of the two cultures about each other. This collection, limited to the cinema of glasnost and the last years of the Soviet Union, is intended to fill one gap. Once again, the film critics lead the way.

We have documented in *The Zero Hour: Glasnost and Soviet Cinema in Transition* (Princeton University Press, 1992) how important cinema was to the Gorbachev period of restructuring, from 1985 to 1991, the year the Soviet Union finally dissolved. This present text is in a sense a companion to *The Zero Hour* for it covers the same time span but goes beyond the camera to focus on the role and reaction of Russian film critics to the shattering changes of the glasnost era. In the twenty-three assembled reviews and essays, some commissioned for this project and almost all appearing in English for the first time, we have attempted to bring the English-speaking audience an accurate picture of the scope and depth of Russian film criticism, written as history was being made on a day-by-day basis around the writers.

These essays then, inevitably, are dispatches from the front, from the heat of the excitement, confusion, questioning, frustration, and reflection that is the essence of living through these times of sharp political, social, cultural, and personal change in Russia. None of the essays is weighted down by footnotes and references to Metz, Derrida, Foucault, and Baudrillard, or even Russia's own Eisenstein and Bakhtin; they reflect something more than intellectual speculations on film. They capture the spirit and the flavor of the times. And despite their differences of approach, each suggests the active engagement of a critic coming to grips with cinema in an age of shifting standards and values.

### "To scorch with words the hearts of men": The Russian critical tradition

The engagement of the Russian film critics was clearly generated by Gorbachev's policy of glasnost. But on a deeper level, it is a product of the Russian critical perspective in general. To sketch roughly: It occupies a middle distance between what in the United States is seen as pop journalistic film reviewing and highbrow theoretical academic analysis. Soviet criticism covers a much more spacious area, one that spreads far beyond film, art, and even culture onto life itself.

The roots of such a perspective must be traced back at least to the first half of the nineteenth century, when literature, and criticism as an equal part of it, became a vital force in the social life of Russia. We should especially consider Alexander Pushkin (who, as Lev Karakhan's essay reminds us, defined the writer's mission as "to scorch with words the hearts of men") and Vissarion Belinsky, the renowned literary critic of the 1830s and 1840s who influenced more than any other writer or rebel of that time both Russian culture and the democratic movement. Since then, a critic has been considered a judge, a teacher, a prophet, or even something of an anarchist, but nothing less. "Intervene in life, for you can change it" became the motto of Russian artists and critics. The critic came to be seen as a medium who should pose and answer basic questions of life and death for ordinary mortals.

In part, this tradition helps us understand why almost none of the essays in this book speaks in analytical detail about the cinematic qualities of the films. Rather, the unspoken center of attention is that of the forces – cultural, political, social – that have given rise to the film itself. Thus, Yuri Bogomolov and Alexander Timofeevsky are both concerned with the issues of democracy (and why it is not happening in Russia) while reflecting on, respectively, the popular genres and the cultural generations. From different positions, both critics arrive at the conclusion that an antiindividualist, collectivist mentality is the root of authoritarian rule.

The times of glasnost have only deepened this trend of general "existentialist" analysis by assigning artistry to a back seat and bringing the search for truth to the limelight.

## "The most important art": The Soviet critical tradition

Along with the Russian cultural tradition, we must also look back at Soviet history, which since the late 1920s has been taming this tradition and succeeded, in fact, quite well. During Stalin's and then Brezhnev's epochs, criticism lost its literal meaning, as personal opinions were dangerously unwise. Criticism was converted into glorifying the "requisite" works and bashing "alien," "harmful" ones, which usually meant death or repression to their creators. Besides the loss of dignity and sincerity, this policy brought about almost total amnesia concerning the basic aesthetic principles that are indispensable to any elementary criticism.

The result of such a Stalinist mentality was not long in coming: The dominant mode of Soviet criticism became "social problem writing," as opposed to structuralism, formalism, auteurism, or any other "sinister '-ism.' " It is not that theoretical and close analysis of film did not exist in the Soviet Union; it is just that it was the exception, cultivated in academic circles, and not the rule. Yuri Lotman's semiotic studies of cinema were clear examples of such an exception. But writing from Estonia rather than Moscow, Lotman geographically, as well as intellectually, made it clear that such an approach, one that American film theorists in particular would be more in sympathy with, is outside the Russian cultural mainstream.

Who makes this stream "main," who fills this abyss between life and art, using the latter to discuss the former and splicing old liberal and new totalitarian concepts together?

## Who's who in Soviet film criticism

There is but one film school in all of Russia that awards film criticism degrees: the National State Film Institute (VGIK) in Moscow. But very few of the contemporary critics (including those represented here) are VGIK graduates.

Traditionally, Soviet critics have been writers who have turned to film, not students who chose the profession. At least for the last three decades, the two main sources that have provided the film industry with its dedicated card-carrying critics have been journalism and literary/theater criticism. The former's attributes are precision and sharpness of style and perception. The latter equips critics with a broader cultural context. The weakness of both is the same – they come from outside film, not from a background steeped in love and understanding of film.

"Today, there are three generations of film critics in the USSR," wrote the young Soviet critic Victor Matizen in his informative 1990 essay, "What, How, and Where Cinema Is Written About in the USSR." "The elder were brought up under Stalin, the middle-aged under Khrushchev and the younger under Brezhnev. The first consider cinema a business of the state and believe in the absolute values; the second consider cinema the public business, but also believe in the absolute; the third maintain that art is a strictly private business and rely on relativism."*

Since glasnost, the Stalinist generation has lost most of its members and influence. Conversely, the Khrushchevian generation (known also as "sixtiesniks," as it very much belongs to the 1960s) has been gaining under new social and political circumstances.

Khrushchev's rule was a time of great reevaluations and hopes, as well as of a renaissance in spirit and art. Poets cried out their verse on the squares and critics recalled the testaments of their nineteenth-century predecessors. But the movement soon failed. By reversing natural law, the thaw was relieved by frost. Some "sixtiesniks" became *apparatchiks*, some dissidents, others just struggled to retain their dignity.

The 1970s sneaked in surreptitiously. This black hole in time did not bear a new generation compatible with the previous one, but rather begat the youth: skeptical, cynical, and introverted.

Therefore, when *perestroika* started off from above, from the Party, the only real force able and willing to support it from below was the middle-aged generation, the "sixtiesniks." Perestroika gave them the last chance to apply their dreams to reality. Unfortunately, Khrushchevian ideals of "socialist democracy" had become hopelessly obsolete. Besides, a new generation of "glasnost kids" had emerged, having learned from their 1970s stagnant childhood to take nothing for granted. This generation was destined to tell their gurus that they have failed again, as Alexander Timofeevsky's sharp obituary to the "dads" does. This generation was also destined to shape public opinion in the chaos of postperestroika Russia.

If the "sixtiesniks" visionary attitude toward art is delineated in Lev Karakhan's essay "Jobless Prophets," their moralistic stand in criticism is largely a target of Timofeevsky's "The Last Romantics." The "sixtiesniks" assess film mostly from general existentialist frontiers. The new generation, if not aesthetic gourmets, are journalists who long to be postmodern connoisseurs. The "sixtiesniks" still tend to comment on films spiritually, placing them in a wide sociomoral context, to which the reviews of *The Commissar* (1967) by Maya Turovskaya, *Is It Easy to Be Young* (1987) by Lev Anninsky, and *The Days of Eclipse* (1988) by Victor Bozhovich are the brightest examples. Their younger opponents insist on examining aesthetics rather than ideology, as the essays by Tatyana Moskvina, Sergei

*Victor Matizen. "What, How and Where the Cinema Is Written About in the USSR," *Soviet Film*, Moscow, 7 (1990): 16–17, 26.

Dobrotvorsky, Igor Aleinikov, Marina Drozdova, and Alexander Kiselev present. They, as Victor Matizen testifies, "need not to influence others, but to be individually free."

Until glasnost, the "sixtiesniks" had all the grounds to utilize their non-formalist methods, inasmuch as Soviet cinema was largely shapeless and overideologized (Mikhail Yampolsky's opening essay, "Cinema Without Cinema," elaborates on the subject). Since the late 1980s, however, the old tools proved useless to treat such playful features as *Assa* (1987) or *The Needle* (1988), which deal with cultural cliches more than with morals and problems. Hence one of the principles of assembling this collection was to preserve the actual balance between different perspectives but also to push them into "dialogue" and, often, into conflict with one another.

## Magazine circles and journal squares

This conflict between generations as well as between individual critics will be seen as more dramatic if we point out that before and during glasnost there were very few venues where the critics could promulgate their ideas.

In 1990, no more than a dozen film journals and magazines were published in all of the USSR, most of them owned by the state and very few run by public organizations such as the Film Makers' Union. A handful of general and literary publications gave some of their pages to film reviews.

Even when Soviet cinema became virtually decentralized, film criticism remained almost exclusively a Moscow-based phenomenon. This is not to say that film magazines and film reviewing did not exist in Kiev, Alma-Ata, Tbilisi, Riga, or Vilnius – major national film capitals. They existed indeed, but had no influence beyond their local level of consumption. Leningrad, the second largest city in Russia and once the cultural capital of the empire, had until 1991 no regular film publication at all.

The Moscow picture was less than encouraging. At the top of the small pyramid was (and remains) *Iskusstvo kino* (*The Art of Film*), published monthly since 1931 (and since 1989 by the Film Makers' Union). As the thickest, most serious noncommercial journal, *Iskusstvo kino* with its 60,000 copies each issue was read, in the early stages of *glasnost*, by far more people than those reading *Cineaste, Film Quarterly, Cinema Journal, Wide Angle*, and *Camera Obscura* combined in the United States. During the late 1980s, the popularity of *Iskusstvo kino* even increased as the magazine, responding to the readers' thirst for glasnost revelations, published sensational pieces from fields other than film.

Its regular departments would include:

> *The Present and the Screen*. Discussions and essays on the current state of the Soviet film industry.

*World of the Soul* (which first appeared in January 1990). Publications of previously unavailable or banned works by Russian and Western philosophers, sociologists, and psychologists, such as Berdyayev, Merezhkovsky, and Freud.

*Cinema of the 1980s* (or later, *the 1990s*). Reviews, interviews, and portraits of film personalities.

*Theory and History*. Studies of history and theory of Soviet cinema; reviews of the revival houses' favorites; memoirs and documents previously censored.

*Selected Prose*. Writings by Soviet dissidents or previously untranslated foreign authors, including Roger Vadim's and Gérard Depardieu's memoirs and Ira Levin's *Rosemary's Baby*.

*Abroad*. Festival reports, discussions, interviews, and foreign film reviews.

*Plots and Facts*. Documentary prose about the unknown pages in the history of Russian and Soviet culture.

*A Screenplay* yet to be produced.


The second leading film periodical, *Sovetskii ekran* (*Soviet Screen*; since 1992, understandably, known as simply *Ekran* "*Screen*") was always closer to what would be considered in the United States a slick magazine. During 1985–91, it published in one million copies, eighteen times a year, and had a definite pop, star-oriented, large-page, color-illustration layout. If not for its questionable printing quality, *Sovetskii ekran* could be called the Russian equivalent of *Premiere*. Many of its departments were dead ringers of *Premiere*'s *Shot By Shot, In the Works, Short Takes*, and others. One important difference, however, was that the Russian top film lists were voted on not by the critics but by the readers.

The rest of the film publications, aside from a few "cultural" newspapers such as *Literaturnaya gazeta* (*Literary Gazette*) and *Sovetskaya kultura* (*Soviet Culture*) and a handful of thin and unpopular advertising editions such as *Sputnik kinozritelya* (*Filmgoer's Companion*), existed primarily for internal circulation either in academia or in the distribution network.

Critics, almost none of whom could ever afford to be a freelancer, and film buffs routinely complained that the arena for film criticism was as limited during glasnost as it was before. But what did general audiences think?

## Critical mass and the masses

In the preperestroika past, dusty magazines full of lies would pile up at the newsstands, unread and without even a future in recycling. With glasnost the picture has changed radically. To buy a magazine during the late 1980s, one often had to stand in line, as for food, clothing, and other necessities. The most liberal *Moskovskiye novosti* (*Moscow News*) and *Ogonyok* (*Little Flame*), a popular, *Newsweek*-like magazine, for example, sold millions of copies, which were never enough – a fact that suggests that the people saw these democratic forums as their voice.

Film journals and film criticism never did occupy such a high niche. But neither publications nor critics could avoid participating in the "glasnost race" – the race for social, political, historical, and not necessarily artistic, truth. The price they had to pay was the critical analysis itself. The reward, however, seemed much higher: From virtually no relationship with their passionate but unenlightened audience, the Soviet film critics suddenly found themselves back at Pushkin's "ground zero": More than ever engaged, now with the new freedom to accomplish the old mission, to scorch with truth the hearts of readers.

The first part of this collection represents the most popular genre of Soviet film criticism – "problem essays." It signifies the latitude of critical reflection and the sharpness of questions the Soviet critics had to raise and solve for the audiences.

In the second half of this book, the films chosen as perestroika's "top ten" movie hits represent the trends in reviewing as well as in the productions that came to be national social events, not merely artistic and commercial successes. As glasnost broke down barriers and allowed discussion of forbidden subjects, the films have become truly sensational, raising the stakes of their critiques. The films selected for this collection also reflect the range of topics that shook up Russian social quietude. Such topics included the guilty past (*The Cold Summer of '53*), state corruption (*A Forgotten Tune for the Flute*), the domestic mafia (*Assa*), drug abuse (*The Needle*), decay of the family (*Little Vera*), anti-Semitism (*Taxi Blues*), and the Afghan vet problem (*Is It Easy To Be Young?*).

## After glasnost

This collection ends with the official withering away of the Soviet Union. But we have capped the Gorbachev era with Marina Drozdova's polemic farewell to glasnost. Her evaluation of the confusion in the postperestroika, post-Soviet Russia reflects both the frustrations and the hopes for the future.

Since the end of the USSR, the enthusiasm for films that tell the truth and the flood of independent films that reached a level of about 400 features in 1991 appears to be over.* In 1992, fewer than a hundred feature films were made and few of those made it to the Russian screens, which have become crowded with cheap American, Indian, and European films.

With Russian cinema in complete disarray, what role will critics now play?

New film magazines suggest an answer. One of them, *Kino-glaz/Cine Eye*, picking up where the state supported multilanguage *Soviet Film* left off, makes an effort to reach out beyond linguistic and territorial boarders with film news, reviews, interviews, and gossip published in Russian and English. The subtitle of the magazine – "art and business" – is misleading: There is not much art in it and plenty of business, mainly for export. With 30,000 copies per issue, *Cine Eye* has a decidedly commercial, "everything-for-sale" look and feel to it, not unlike a blend of *Variety* and *Premiere*. Although Soviet film magazines always carried photos of female film stars, the actresses represented in *Cine Eye* are blatantly more sexually alluring than in the past – and phone numbers, weight, and height are generously provided by the editors!

Another new periodical, the St. Petersburg–based *Seans* (*Picture Show*) takes an entirely different direction. Openly elitist and bohemian, it writes about David Lynch, postmodern mutants, deconstruction, and recent openings in the same cool and ironic tone that denotes fatigue of the disengaged and disillusioned postpolitical consciousness.

How does this new critical picture relate to the state of cinema?

The film voted Best Film of 1992 by 90 Russian critics was Nikolai Dostal's *Cloud Paradise* (*Oblako-rai* [1992]). What won critics over was the absolute simplicity of the tale of a youth in his late teens who decides to do what nobody else in his tiny village has ever done: to leave the village. Gogol, Beckett, Buñuel, and Chaplin all cross paths in this finely wrought ensemble piece with no special effects, no gimmicks, no rock score, and no orgies.

Perhaps the 1990s without socialism and beyond the shambles of instant capitalism will allow some critics the chance to write with such lucid simplicity. They too may find not Aristophanes' *Cloudcuckooland* but a critical *Cloud Paradise* in which they have the courage to leave their villages and strike out for new territory.

*See Michael Brashinsky. "Nyet And Da," *The Independent*, New York (October 1992): 14–17. Also: Andrew Horton. "Russia," *Film Guide International 1993*, ed. Peter Cowie, London: Hamlyn, 1992, pp. 324–9.

# PART ONE

# Films in a
# shifting landscape

# Cinema without cinema

## Mikhail Yampolsky

As I reread these notes, I fully recognize that not only *a typical Soviet film* but also *Soviet film* overall are categories far from a scientific definition. The films by various directors from different Soviet republics hardly can be measured by the same "yardstick." We all nevertheless intuitively sense that in our film industry, some artistic standard has evolved that appears in some current films as well as in the film-thinking. This standard is shaped by several common cultural traditions and the peculiarities of the film industry and film education in the Soviet Union.

Particular to our cinema is the firm reluctance to divide film production into the two categories used widely abroad. Films in the West tend to either commercial or artistic quality, whereas between these opposites, there is a wide variety of cross-overs and also an obvious tendency toward commercialization of the artistic (even among such masters as Fellini).

Soviet cinema has an abundance of top-notch films, but truly entertaining films for general audiences are utterly weak, as these films are usually produced by second-rate film makers. This situation is easily explained by the fact that Russian and Soviet traditions, more than anything else, scorn popular culture.

The bulk of Soviet production is unappealing to both film buffs and ordinary film goers. From the regular viewer's standpoint, Soviet film is a message to nobody. This paradox is reflected in the genre structure that, although it is quite astonishing, we have grown used to. Commercial cinema cannot exist without active participation of *regular* film genres. Our film industry is truly *genreless* and here it differs from other film industries around the world. However, we are accustomed to speaking of an "industrial film genre." But a *genre* is an established formal mythic system that meets the viewer's deep psychological needs through the stereotypes of perception. That is why commercial film abroad banks on the genre structure. Outside of commercial film, genre language and cliches serve as models for parody and subjects to various formal "inversions."

In Soviet cinema, the "industrial film" is a sort of genre unto itself. Although it has its own specific mythology, it disregards the viewer's interests and preferences, or, in other words, the viewer's psychology. It is

11

not a commercial genre but neither is it art. The range of genre indications in it is far from complete. The same could be said about Soviet comedies, musicals, and thrillers.

The avalanche of films sans audience of course causes alarm. But how this alarm is expressed is another matter. Since the 1920s, the film crisis in the Soviet Union has been interpreted as a script crisis. We constantly try to overcome inertia in the film industry by the magic of screenwriting contests or enticing authors of other media to film. Such prodding never leads to anything solid. Film makers think that the unpopularity of their films is due to flaccid characters, weak narrative, or pale subject matter. Even if this is partly true (our scripts are hardly the best), the attitude speaks for itself. The responsibility for the trouble in our film is being put upon *words* as opposed to *images*.

I have not heard a single complaint about insufficiency of film language. Soviet film mentality is essentially *logocentric*.

Our films traditionally focus on the problems of the hero's psychology, the nature of social conflicts or narrative collisions – aspects that belong entirely to the *literary bases* of film. Not accidentally, a whole slew of literary critics earn a tidy sum in film criticism: Anninsky, Rassadin, Runin, and others. Soviet film criticism compared to film criticism abroad is hardly interested in cinematic qualities, and is as logocentric as the films themselves.

Here the influence of our word-focused cultural tradition is felt. Russian culture is verbal rather than visual. However, the commercial success of a film hinges on its ability to cause hypnotic sensual reactions in the audience, and the literary components of film are least capable of creating that mesmerizing effect.

Contemporary film theory assumes that the commercial success of a film rests on the film's ability to give the viewer a specific pleasure. Behind this assumption turn the wheels of complex film devices such as *identification*. Unfortunately, our film critics have not given this subject any attention. We often proceed from the outdated notion that the viewer identifies only with the film's protagonist. But contemporary science knows that identification is twofold. Science distinguishes between primary identification, the psychological connection with the spectacle on the screen as a whole, and secondary identification with a character. Moreover, the latter is based on the former. In order to project him- or herself onto the protagonist, the viewer must already be engrossed in the film's world. In Soviet cinema, primary identification is remarkably weak, even though it should serve as the foundation for enjoyment of the film. Our films have no hypnotizing effect on the viewer's consciousness. To create this magic one must be fluent in film language.

Among the essential elements of primary identification are the darkness of the theater and the blinking beam of light overhead – components of any film screening, which establish the conditions for submerging the viewer in that dreamlike state that accompanies the normal perception of a film. These are not the only components. No less important is the sensual contact with the world on screen created by the richness of sight and sound, the rhythmic structures, and so on.

The lack of attention to these elements is often explained by the technological backwardness of Soviet film industry. This is partly accurate. The absence of professional sound equipment (Nagras) or inferior quality of film stock explains the sloppiness of interior shots or synchronization in our films. Semiotically, these particulars of film production take on special significance. The shortage of high-speed film stock dulls the visual atmosphere and blurs the boundaries of light and shadow as well as the nuances of color that cast the magic of film. The inadequacy of syncs also affects the plausibility of the screen world.

The ease, however, with which our directors approach the situation and march toward failure is amazing. As a result, they cannot achieve the full illusion of reality even on location. Why deny it: the barns in our films look less real than the spaceships in *Star Wars*. In fact, this is caused by the replacement of the visual and audio dimensions (that is, cinematic dimensions) by the verbal one. With tremendous artistic and financial waste, verbosity is killing our films.

Apparently, the technological lag in this case has its roots not only in technical backwardness, but also in the mentality of our film makers. Even for those who fully understand the significance of sensory elements, the process of integrating these elements into the film reflects the logocentric "ideology." *The Kiss* (1983) by Roman Balayan, an extremely talented film maker, provides a good example. Trying to convey the sensation of heat on the screen, Balayan recorded the sound of mosquitos buzzing. But he mixed it with such volume that the sound that should have worked subliminally stood out from the background like the roar of a jet, overpowering the intended effect. *Dragging the subconscious to the conscious level begets many of the troubles in Soviet film.*

The best of our film makers tend to trust only the "full-volume," totally verbalized material. Even Tarkovsky, that remarkable master of visual expression, seemed often to distrust himself, overshadowing the magic of his imagination with flowery literary phrases.

This constant striving for verbalization more often than not censors that which is too frightening to be revealed to the public. I think that the almost statutory ban on erotica and violence in our films is not incidental to our worship of the spoken word. Although I do not propose introducing naturalism into our films, I do think that it would not hurt to subject Soviet film to a thorough psychoanalysis.

All of the foregoing fully relates to another lack in our cinema, that of a secondary level of identification with the characters. As noted, the accent has traditionally been placed on psychological depiction. In this sense, our cinema operates on two unsubstantiated beliefs. The first assumes that the viewer expects an idealized screen hero with whom he or she can identify. The second dictates that the viewer looks for complex psychological role patterns. Of course, to meet these demands of the viewer, screenwriters are expected to come to the rescue. However even a cursory glance at world cinema will show that the viewers identify most strongly with actors with a certain magnetism, not quite intellectual. Humphrey Bogart, James Dean, Marlene Dietrich, and Brigitte Bardot rarely created deep psychological roles on screen. Rather, it appears that maximum identification can be achieved through an actor who possesses not only an unusual personality, but also some erotic allure. I mean eroticism in the broadest sense, as Béla Balázs used this term in the 1920s: not as unbridled sex or pornography, but rather as the normal sensual attraction we feel toward the face and body as rendered on the screen largely with the help of special lighting and body language. I think that it is worth reexamining Eisenstein, who consciously used erotic elements even in *Battleship Potemkin*. Thus, he admitted using the structure of a love triangle in the film's narrative.

It is shocking how erotica was eradicated from Soviet films with an iron fist as though it were something alien or hateful to us. Furthermore, the persecution of erotica is part of the general persecution of sensual elements in film and can be interpreted as an example of the verbal/visual dichotomy we have discussed.

Soviet actors have a tough row to hoe. They are forced to use all of their acting ability to compensate for that which is purposely suppressed or ignored by directors. As a result a strange syndrome has developed, characterized by hysterical acting, which is nothing short of the actors' sublimation of the screen's lack of erotica. We are all well acquainted with the standard scenes of yelling and hysterics in our films. It is notable that these scenes are most commonly seen in "industrial films" in which the ubiquitous foreman in grungy coveralls collapses into hysterics on the phone demanding more cement. Battle-fatigued officers in war movies scream in a similar manner into field telephones when demanding ammunition.

The similarity of Soviet war films and "industrial films" is significant and not accidental. The authoritarian style of economic management, still flourishing, was adopted directly by industry from the military. There is more to it. A normally functioning factory is not a good source of dramatic conflict. To give an "industrial film" a more interesting plot, the narrative develops as if there were a war. During the years when our society was portrayed as blissful and idyllic, war was the main source of conflict and is so to this day.

Back to our screaming factory foreman: I do not know if industrial discussions are so emotional in real life. But in the movies, the telephone clearly becomes a symbol of distance and nonphysical contact, and the hysterical scream seems to announce the absence of normal human relations. There must be less screaming in all the films of the world than in a dozen Soviet "industrial films"!

A film's popularity is directly related to its underlying mythology. A strong subcurrent of mythology almost always flows through a commercial film. Only when the archetypes of a viewer's subconscious are evoked can the viewer totally become immersed in the film. The stunning success of Lucas's and Spielberg's epics proves this. All of the recent box office hits have quite consciously exploited ancient mythology. Again, it would be worth referring to Eisenstein, who attached great significance to archetypes. The preponderance of mythology in commercial cinema casts doubt on a typical assumption: that audiences can be attracted by making characters more complex and by sharpening social commentary.

Of course, the extraordinary timeliness of a film such as Tengiz Abuladze's *Repentance* (1984) can attract great numbers. But today's director cannot depend on the perpetual discovery of formerly forbidden subjects.

The well-established film genres – Western, thriller, science fiction – all rely on strong myths. It is not that Soviet cinema lacks a mythology, but that we usually slink away from the question. The basic Soviet film pantheon was formed in the 1930s and still carries the mark of that period and of the ideology of Stalinism. It is particularly noticeable in contemporary films. Overcoming these mythological constructs is an unavoidable step in the process of overhauling Soviet cinema. It is unavoidable for film critics as well.

In the 1930s our mythology was quite effective and guaranteed success; viewers' expectations and social myths matched. Like almost every modern mythological framework that grew out of the Judeo-Christian tradition, the myths of the 1930s invariably painted a bright conflictless future, a golden era, and a solution to all contradictions. Reaching this glorious future demands a sacrifice by the hero who has to be initiated into the ranks of the worthy. The hero comes forward and undergoes various trials and tribulations: He must battle an enemy (a member of the White Guard or a saboteur), the elements (typical in an initiation rite), fire (in "industrial films"), earth (in "collective farm films"), or water (the motif of a flood or sailing). As a result, utopia was granted (the climax of most films), and the hero was declared a savior, demigod, or "man of the future."

Such a mythology, of course, was used to strengthen the ideology of the Stalinist cult, with its typical myth of superhero, personal sacrifice, and heroism securing the future heaven. The same mythology reflected the popular belief in the swift and miraculous coming of the "Golden Age." It also justified exorbitant human sacrifices. Only the "mystical sacrifice" in this mythological construct is capable of ensuring heaven on earth. It is of the utmost significance that this mythology was rooted in the ancient archetypes of folk consciousness.

This mythology, somewhat altered, is preserved in our current films. We still think along the lines of hero/sacrifice and the need for a redeemer from the boss's office, of battling the elements, even when the subject is modern manufacturing or agriculture.

Without evaluating how harmful or helpful such a mythology is (personally, I think the harm far outweighs the benefit today), let us note only the ever-dwindling relevance of it to the modern-day social myths. Fewer and fewer people believe in the magical possibility of achieving that bright shining future, and fewer still are willing to pay the price of a permanent sacrifice. Thank God that belief in a messiah has evaporated. Due to the new ecological consciousness, even less popular is the belief in the effectiveness of fighting with nature. The old Soviet film mythology has come into sharp conflict with the new youth culture that is developing completely different myths whether we like it or not. For some youth, the idea of a golden era is less likely than the end of the world or complete chaos. Films that preserve the unaltered set of traditional dogma drive young audiences away from the cinema.

It is worth noting that myths are tied to irrational elements in our psyches. We have till now been afraid to address this point, relying instead on the power of our rationality. I want to be understood correctly: I am not advocating that we eliminate rational elements from our cinema, and I certainly do not mean to cut out sharp social commentary of complex characters. I am merely calling attention to the fact that on the deepest and most basic level, film, like the other arts and perhaps more so, is connected to the unconscious structures of our psyche. We cannot ignore this fact any more, especially when we strive for commercial success. We cannot ignore it, too, because, despite our cult of the obvious and of the verbal, the cinematic mind unconsciously recreates old myths, cliches, and stereotypes.

★ ★ ★

I have only addressed a fraction of the problems facing our film industry here. These problems are too complex to pretend to solve at one sitting. They demand serious study. In the meantime, our film critics tiptoe around them, relegating them to the dark recesses of the critical mind. It is time to fearlessly and soberly tackle these problems that have till now been kept at arm's length. It is naive to suppose that because we do not acknowledge problems, they do not exist.

Decisive steps must be taken to change the direction of thinking among our film makers. Our film studies and film making programs should play an important role here. And, finally, we must hammer home a few banal truths. It is important to understand that film is not only character, plot, and conflict transferred onto celluloid, but that it is also a dance of light, space, sound, face and body on the screen. Only having adopted these simple truths and having understood the deeper workings of cinema can our directors finally create films that are interesting to watch.

Despite all the sins of our screenwriters, it is time to realize that the infamous script crisis is simply a reflection of a deeper crisis in Soviet film as a whole.

# Cinema for every day

*Yuri Bogomolov*

Yevgeny Zamyatin once wrote about the 1920s: "It's hard to repair a water pipe, and it's hard to build a house, but it is easy to build a Tower of Babel."

It is very much the same today. Or at least it is similar. Great projects and enormous plans are all over, but there are still no films about our everyday life. Such films can perform the functions of folklore, that is, cultivate the reflexes of kindness, courage, justice, humaneness. But there are no more than one or two such movies today.

Every such success comes as a gift of fortune, just like a repaired water pipe.

In the past twenty years, successes of this sort could be counted on the fingers of one hand: *Moscow Does Not Believe in Tears, The Crew, The Meeting Place Cannot Be Changed*, and *The Cold Summer of '53*. Probably I could recall a few more, but they would not change the picture.

Some reservations are to be made before going any further. Although defending a functioning water pipe, I am not against the construction of a Tower of Babel. I am not against Lofty Art, of course, but I think that Lofty Art is really a gift from heaven.

But the construction of a habitable, warm, cinematic home is within the potential of people who live on earth.

The necessity of such a home today is more keen than it seemed not long ago. It turns out that the level of humaneness is appallingly low, unfortunately, not just among film makers, but also among writers and scientists. If the overwhelming majority of the Soviet population votes against the abolition of capital punishment, it means that the humanistic potential of our society is reduced to zero.

At the Fifth Film Makers' Union Congress, we told our Emperor (the bureaucratic apparatus of film authorities) decisively and with confidence that he was naked.

Then this truth was verified by the march of events. We saw that the *state* as a notion was not identical with *society*, and that this state as an institution has turned into a kind of Hoffmann's Zahes the Little, whose power on us became menacingly total. We began to realize the necessity for the sovereignty of an individual, for the spiritual autonomy of each person. Today, Zahes the Little is out of grace here. The naked emperor has been dethroned. What will happen next?

We have found out what we were afraid to admit to ourselves: Subjection to the naked emperor has impoverished our spiritual and emotional abilities. A chained watchdog is self-assured and impudent; it growls. But the same dog unchained wags its tail. Left on its own, it loses its confidence. A chain, as we have learned, not only binds motion, it gives strength to a watchdog. We still feel quite uncomfortable without our chains.

That is why we tend to fall into either uneasy irritation or dreadful apathy. That is why we initiate things that we can never finish, dig new foundations for structures that we will never be able to erect.

*Perestroika* has brought a sense of mental and social homelessness to many people, including film makers and their audiences. Just take a look at the movies now playing. I will not touch on their *artistic* qualities, because their subject matter speaks for itself.

If we consider *Assa* (1989), *Little Vera* (1988), *Temptation* (1988), *Baby Doll* (1988), *Tragedy in Rock* (1988), *The Needle* (1988), or the already notorious *King of Crime* (1988), we would see only different variations of the same formula: A man (or a woman as in *Little Vera* [1988]) is forced to become an outsider, a person on the verge of disaster, suspended in midair. The idea of a home is not even about to materialize before this hopeless person who clings to whatever or whoever happens to be there.

Some take refuge in drugs, others in rock 'n' roll. Carmen from Yuri Kara's *King of Crime* finds protection in the mob. But all these harbors are clearly accidental and unreliable. The bottom line here, as we can see it, is that an individual is not prepared for individualized life. He can not walk by himself like Kipling's cat. The young heroine of *Baby Doll* tries to be herself after having been kicked out of a gymnastics team, this machine for generating state prestige, and fails.

In accordance to the standards of our communal existence, individualism has always been cursed as filthy here, as some kind of leprosy. Today, it is a backbreaking burden to carry.

Charlie Chaplin comes to mind. He truly was like Kipling's cat. Neither the state nor any social institution had the power to assimilate or integrate the Tramp. The police, army, and the moral majority all ganged up on Charlie and, despite their immense structure, recoiled from this man who seemed so tiny. Although a tramp, he managed to strike his audience as a settled man, someone with a home. The secret was that his home was inside him.

"Their" Western inveterate individualist, it turned out, was more sturdy than "our" chronic collectivist. And this is the key to understanding why freedom comes so hard for us.

r as I know, one of the principal problems in creating a legitimate
that of giving equal rights to individuals and to the state itself.
Generally, the majority dominates over the individual, which is true about
the modern Western world as well. But while in the West, this domination
has proceeded in a democratic way, in our country, it has taken the form
of dictatorship.

Understandably, the Stalinist regime of uncontrolled power of one
masked itself as the power of the masses. Of course, this situation did not
develop out of nowhere. The crowds dominated in the October Communist Revolution as much as in the February Bourgeois Revolution. But the
individual was not lost. Personality still retained its value; it did not become a zero and then turn into trash.

Then art began to glorify and promote the ideas of collectivism (although those who were behind the movement – Mayakovsky, Eisenstein,
Meyerhold – were great individuals).

Individuality broke down when our revolution became permanent. The
Civil War turned into the norm for everyday life. The rest of our history
reflects a heroic fight of the masses against the alien, individualistic mentality, with one universal remedy – collectivization.

To me, perestroika was an attempt to free each of us from the dictate of
the collective mass. Not from collectivism as it is, but from its tyrannic
oppression. Not from the *power* but from the *dictatorship* of *us* over *I*. In
film, we should involve ourselves in deliberate and consistent cultivation
of a taste for individual freedom and responsibility, personal wealth, and
generosity.

We have been discussing democratization of film making. This is an
important matter. But another side of it is equally important: democratization of our spiritual and intellectual life.

In a speech at the opening of one of his films, director Stanislav Govorukhin touched upon the topic of commercial success. He referred to wom-
en's magic pantyhose that could assume the color of a dress they were
worn with. There is a great demand for such chameleon pantyhose, so
their black-market price in Odessa is astronomical. Govorukhin assured
the audience that it would be no problem to him to make a chameleon
film if he so chooses.

Without devaluating his words, I would like to remark: The cinema that
the critics call popular (and every bit of it always fits into one genre or
another) does not simply adjust to the tastes of the audiences (let alone
strictly commercial expectations); instead, it ventures into the collective
subconscious desires.

Not long ago, I thought that making a good genre film requires nothing
but calculation. Now I know that a successful film for a mass audience is
an irrational achievement that calls for intuition and inspiration.

Stanislav Govorukhin has succeeded once in this, in his *Meeting Place*

*Cannot Be Changed* (1979). Overall, however, collective subconscious has hardly been addressed yet in the Soviet Union.

Recently, we had an opportunity to experience cinema for the masses.

*Escriva Isaura* (1989), a maudlin Brazilian soap opera, was shown in prime time television at the height of perestroika with tremendous success. This success could be expected, I dare say. What really surprised me was that much of the audience considered the film true to reality.

How could one expect such an artificial fairy tale to be taken for bare truth? But, on the other hand, how could it be otherwise, for there was no dividing line between the Imaginary and the Real within the limits of our past collective subconscious that Stalin's ideologists successfully used for decades. That is why the rich screen lies in Ivan Pyriev films were taken in those days for reality by the people whose own hunger seemed to them like an illusion, a mirage, a shadow.

Substitution of the Real by the Unreal is much easier done in the consciousness of the masses than in the mind of an individual.

Many critics, including me, have exhausted themselves by writing and speaking about the misadventures of Isaura. This series has not a jot of artistic value, but it is clearly of scholastic interest as a mythological reflection of the suppressed instincts of the masses.

Take a look at *Isaura*. There are two worlds there: the world of the slaves and the world of the rich. Isaura is well educated and refined, but she is a slave. Her social status is split: She is sitting between two chairs. As for the narrative, instead of unfolding, it swings from one freedom to another, from a pillory at the *fasenda* to the estate of the rightful owner. When Isaura gets an opportunity to trade places with her master, she rejects it.

When the billion-member Soviet audience chose to share the swinging experiences with Isaura, it admitted to the deep complex of nonfreedom and inequality in the subconscious of our "democratic" society.

*Isaura* touched a vital nerve. Evidently, myths are created somewhere at the bottom of the collective subconscious, in the archaic layers that accumulate ancient instincts from tribal man. In those layers, myths assume the air of vague haziness of clouds; from time to time they descend like heavy rains.

The consciousness of the Soviet mass audience is controlled by mythologies, inborn and acquired. That is why our myths can hardly be successful or even understood in other parts of the world. I suspect that Western viewers were busy consuming *Isaura* as well, but not with such an appetite as we have experienced here.

The state of nonfreedom is more powerful in our country than we could imagine or would like to believe.

I recall the fantastic success of the legendary *Tarzan* (1932) that swept the Soviet Union right after the war. This sequence of *Tarzan* movies reverberated through the minds of the postwar generation so strongly that it became part of our "family values." Tarzan, this primitive individual, a jungle citizen, made a deep impression on the solid consciousness of the Soviet people. He subversively stimulated the hidden desire of the Soviets for individualism.

Authorities lamented for years that our children did not want to play Chapayev, Maxim, or Chkalov, the legendary heroes of the first Soviet myths. Now we can open up the secret why they played Tarzan and then Fantomas, a French comics character, instead. Both Tarzan and Fantomas presented the patterns for primitive individualism. Chapayev, Chkalov, and Maxim were of a different kind: Generals leading the troops rather than individualists, they embodied and personified the group.

Every age forms its own mythological climate. Brezhnev's stagnation period reflected itself in our collective subconscious in its own way. Take the hit 1970s' television miniseries, *Seventeen Moments of Spring* (1973). When Isayev, the Soviet intelligence officer, penetrated the Gestapo, hiding under the name of Stirlitz, most of us imagined ourselves as Stirlitz in appearance and Isayev at heart. The masquerade in Hitler's headquarters meant the revolt of heroic romanticism against the conformist complex. Judging by the tremendous success of *Seventeen Moments*, this complex had become a solid factor in the mass consciousness.

Stirlitz was a myth that offered an escape, emotionally if not in any other way. Detective Zheglov from *The Meeting Place Cannot Be Changed* was a different myth, which served the same purpose of leading the audiences away from their daily routine. Many contemporary films aim at that goal. The results, however, are often problematic. *Frozen Cherry*, for example, centers on a woman who has to choose between badly organized living (which she shares with her sweetheart) and a settled existence (with a handsome man who does not seem to care about her). Eventually she chooses an unsettled version, but in doing so, she is forced into a serious emotional crisis.

Another woman, a prostitute in *Intergirl* (1989), sacrifices everything including her reputation, her body, and her soul to a different way of life: She marries a foreigner and moves to Sweden, where she does not belong. If the movie hits the box office, it will be primarily due to the audience's attraction to that "different way of life." Therefore, we will be able to conclude that the importance of enslaving the slave's life has risen here to paramount proportions.

I would also like to know how the Soviet audience will react to be *Dark Eyes* (1987). The success of the film in the West is easily understandable. It is a story of a European bourgeois who goes on a spree in nonbourgeois Russia. What appeals here, most likely, is a totally bourgeois crossing of three auras: Chekhov's (the original story), mysterious Russia, and the aging Marcello Mastroianni.

But soil is different here, and so is the climate. We are ridden by an

inferiority complex every time we compare ourselves to the Western bour-
geoisie. A bourgeois experience seems exotic to us; we see it as a kind of
a Western–Oriental sect. That is why I do not believe that European bourgeois reflections could touch our collective soul.

As for *The King of Crime*, the film is a megahit. And I dare say that it is
not bad taste that makes it successful, but the right keys to the secret subconscious interests of the mass audience that the film makers have found.
By that I mean the concern with social vulnerability of an individual, his
inability to change his pitiful daily life.

These movies are only three cards taken out of a full deck.

We can be as ironic and condescending about the popular cinema as
we wish, but it is impossible to move on without this kind of film. After
all, it is hopeless to try to build a Tower of Babel without a working water
pipe.

Now, back to the collision between Lofty Art and Popular Culture. Russian critic Vissarion Belinsky wrote about it a century and a half ago. Even
before that, a certain European addressed it in relation to the prebourgeois
revolution of Peter the Great. "If a sovereign will not bring up a manufac-
turer who is capable of weaving such fine broadcloth that mounts in its
value up to one quina a yard, then less possible is it for an astronomer to
be brought up in his state."

The dramatic nature of perestroika is bound to the search for spiritual
autonomy. This autonomy frightens and attracts at the same time. I remember military demobilization after World War II. It was a happy and
horrifying moment. It was happy because we did not need to move in ranks
any more. And it was horrifying because from now on we would have to
take care of our own lives and we would be responsible for every step we
took.

There was a fear of civilian life. There was a cowardly wish to stay for
additional service.

The sedition and agitation that we observe and feel today are connected
with hunger, and fear of the general decollectivization, and with the lack
of the capacity for individualization.

Clearly, there are many of us who want to stay "for additional service."
Especially those who do not know how to do anything else but to give
orders or carry them out. Street nationalism as well as vulgarly theoretical
nationalism are but two kinds of additional service in the agonizing system.

An instinctive yearning for the collective "us" is on the side of corpo-
rations and bureaucracy. The difficulty that perestroika faces in the spiritual sphere is a difficulty of transforming *us* into *I*.

But God save us from being tempted again by the idea of permanent
revolution, the idea that would end up establishing total domination of
Lofty Art and "author's cinema," and exiling the mass culture.

# The last romantics

*Alexander Timofeevsky*

The term "movement of the 1960s" (or "sixtiesniks") is used frequently and with assurance, even though it would be as difficult to define as "national character." Although the "movement" expressed itself primarily in the arts, its members had never published a manifesto, unlike futurists, symbolists, or any other artistic group. Unity of creative program had nothing to do with our "movement." In fact, any kind of unity would be hard to apply to that generation. And lastly, what generation was that?

The only common denominator left to justify the "movement" would lie in the sphere of ideas and feelings. Clearly, we are approaching slippery ground here. Not everybody who lived and worked in the 1960s shared the same thoughts and emotions. Not all of the "sixtiesniks" who live and work today are still inspired by the ideals of that time. This writer by no means claims to be scientifically accurate in his definitions. As a representative of another generation, he could in no way retain objectivity. Having protected ourselves with these reservations, let us finally examine the subject itself.

★ ★ ★

The anti-Stalinist attitude is the first self-defined prerogative of the 1960s movement. Its members call themselves "the children of the 20th Party Congress" (1956) at which Khrushchev officially denounced Stalinism. However, the name is not exact. If those "children" existed at all, they could have been born, like myself, only after the Congress. All those who found a tribune in the 1960s, whatever age they were at the time, are children of Stalin's thirty-year regime, which is as important to realize as it is to recognize their anti-Stalinist zeal. Therefore, we must first try to outline some generic traits of the Stalin's era.

The prevailing quality of the period was ritualization. In one of the aesthetic declarations of the time, the film *Oath* (1937), which levels the secondary social mythology of the time and the primary, classical one, there is a staggering scene. Two agriculturists argue about who won the best harvest contest. The winner will be bathed with ritualistic honors.

24

With no trouble, they agree that the competition was won by Him (Stalin), and it is He who must be bathed. A montage sequence follows in which we see the bottom of a canal covered with gigantic portraits of Stalin: He is being "bathed." Such high dependence of personal success on the will of the One (Stalin), such literal identification of substance with a visual image of it, let alone the most ritualistic act of bathing, were previously known only in prehistoric pagan societies. The culture that engages in such a real, powerful, and primitive ritual has no time for everyday life.

The style of Stalinist art in the 1930s–50s has withered from classicism to mannerism. Something cracked in Stalin's utopia after the war. The statue of Nike of Samothrace, striving for victory, thrusting forward and only forward, could have been (as it was before) the emblem of the time. Strict classicism of the 1930s accepted only the heroic, high genres: landscape and still life were persecuted as the enemies of the people; even a fable sounded like an ode; even a comedy ended like an epic. Grigori Alexandrov, a film maker remarkably sensitive to the style of the epoch, expressed this perhaps better than anyone else in the grandiose finales of *The Circus* (1936), *Volga, Volga* (1938), and *The Bright Path* (1940).

Alexandrov was also the first to capture the new trend after the war. There is no ritualistic apotheosis in his *Spring* (1946). The film does not have a striking ideological message; it plays like a slightly reshaped Hollywood screwball comedy, quite different from Alexandrov's prewar works. In *Volga, Volga*, Strelka, a mailwoman, grows into a famous composer who visits the Kremlin in a limo. The story is that of Cinderella who gets her prince as a dowry rather than reward. In contrast, the lead of *Spring*, a scientist, played by the same actress, Liubov Orlova, is a respectable woman, content with her matrimonial life. No fairy-tale miracles happen in her new universe.

The reason is not that the people who survived the war became tired of utopias and desired nothing but ordinary life. The reason is that any utopia, being monstrous by nature, has, thank God, a short breath.

At Stalin's "DisneyWorld," VDNH (the National Exhibit of Economic Progress), fertility was symbolized by priapic sculptures of oxen. The fountains there immortalized plants and flowers that were shaped like penises and vaginas. Together with such symbols as the bathing of an icon, discussed before, all the inadvertent manifestations of primitive mythology eventually debilitated the Stalinist utopia. Primitive mythology in the postwar twentieth century was too unnatural even for such an unnatural mentality as that of Stalinism. As Chekhov used to say, every disgrace must have its own proprieties. Quietly but firmly, the culture returned to family life and values. Even though *Spring* has no family life in the true sense of the word, there is indeed a dream of such. Hence, the main difference between *The Bright Path* and *Spring* is not in their realities as much as in their ideals, which makes it even more striking.

The fancy apartments in *Spring* had nothing to do with the communal boxes where the moviegoers huddled, sharing the utilities. But those apartments had everything to do with what the moviegoers wanted to see and dreamed about. The Future in postwar Stalinist aesthetics was projected onto the Present, human and cozy; the Present, good for enjoyable living and not just for stormy construction of communism.

The French idea of "salon" aesthetics describes this new cozy dream quite well. And although the weight of the "salon" should not be exaggerated (ritual still dominated the arts at the time), the fact that the idea has appeared points up the crisis.

That is why with all due respect to the courage of Nikita Khrushchev and his sensational report to the Twentieth Party Congress, we must admit that he did no more than any other reformer would have done in his place. Khrushchev was not about to abolish the utopia; all he wanted was to pour new wine into old jugs. The operation had to be performed by the intelligentsia of the 1960s, which quickly realized the social expectations.

The change did not come without paradoxes, at least three of them.

Firstly, Khrushchev disliked and feared the intelligentsia, unreasonably indeed, of which the sadly ludicrous case of the film *Ilyich Square* (1963) is a good example. It would be hard to imagine a more Soviet, more communist, more Khrushchevian picture. The director Marlen Khutsiev performed rejuvenation of old wine with talent and honesty. It is well known how Khrushchev paid him back: The film, centered around the generation-gap problem, was shelved, harshly reedited and released under a new title, *I Am Twenty*, only in 1965.

Secondly, the intelligentsia who radically opposed Stalinism, but not the Communist state and government, immortalized the utopia as they confused cause with effect. The cult of revolutionary art of the 1920s, as frightfully utopian as the Stalinist art, outlived many other Soviet myths mainly thanks to the "sixtiesniks."

The third paradox is the most dramatic. Longing for democracy, the intellectuals of the 1960s had unwillingly ruined its only hope – the idea of a Soviet "salon" that, like any other "salon," opposes the totalitarian Utopia, focusing on the individual rather than the collective. A romantic dream of community – the core for any utopia or any fascism – is the most dreadful threat to democracy. Champions of the new romantic community, the "sixtiesniks" fought recklessly against what they called "philistine comfort" and we called "salon." God knows, they had not a slightest idea of what they were doing.

In the beginning of Khrushchev's "thaw," the intelligentsia worshiped the revolution. Even though some of them would change their minds later, there was, in fact, a strong inner resemblance between the 1920s and the 1960s.

Both generations started from scratch, from ground zero. For both generations, the Present as historical, cultural, spiritual, and even physical force was replaced by the Future. Both generations dreamed of utopian community. Both believed in the inevitably happy reforms, based on total enlightenment. ("We'll all live happily ever after if everyone (a) learns to read (1920s), (b) learns to read Solzhenitsyn (1960s).") Both generations fought against the philistines, against the material and for the spiritual. Both sacrificed aesthetics to ethics. Both were ascetic, and morally and intellectually intolerant.

However, the roots of the 1920s and the 1960s breeds were disparate. So were the kinds of intolerance. Ideologists of the 1920s tried very hard to demolish the old world and they succeeded. Old morals went down the drain along with everything "old." The horror of Stalinism was not only that millions of people were exterminated, but that both hangmen and victims accepted their destinies as given. The Ten Commandments were desecrated and forgotten. Resurrection of the Ten Commandments was the major task for "sixtiesniks." It was more their misfortune than their fault that, being the children of their time, they did not know any better way to do it than to create a moral utopia.

That utopia (like any utopia, a product of abstract thinking) reduced the multitude of moral codes – political, religious, social, private – to one common denominator: truth, as abstract, as it was overwhelming and compelling. Truth was perceived as the sole purpose of art; artists were seen as the missionaries of Truth. On the altar of Truth, Solzhenitsyn's revelations could be replaced by a Hemingway novel, or Mikhail Romm's film *Nine Days of One Year* (1961); this would not change the absolute nature of the icon. The "sixtiesniks" would force poor Marya Ivanovna, the character in the Romm film, into reading Erich Maria Remarque; they would torment a militiaman with Hemingway, honestly believing that this would make them better. That a militiaman may have his own moral guidelines that could be valid without intersecting with Hemingway's seemed unthinkable to the "sixtiesniks." That Marya Ivanovna could improve her morals by not having to push her way through the grocery lines and not by watching Fellini was out of the question.

Democracy based on a moral absolute – the whimsical dream of authoritarian mentality – lay in the foundation of the 1960s' utopia to which plurality was a foreign and incomprehensible notion.

The confusion of art and truth is what we are and will be paying for by having to see journalistic film collages such as *The Incident on a Regional Scale* (1988). In a healthy culture, art must obey its own laws. Art must be artful, whereas truthful must be a newspaper, appropriately named "Pravda" (Truth).

Anatoly Strelyanyi, in his remarkable article "The Last Romantic," showed how Khrushchev was going to revolutionize the economy morally. The intelligentsia stood by its leader, but the authorities did not. The sociopolitical apparatus resisted the moral absolute. It had other plans. It was going to freeze in grand stagnation. The conflict was ripening, and our heroes, having to face the failure of the utopian project along with the confrontation with the authorities, split.

A totally new period was on its way, a period of dissidents. Everyone had to take sides in the universal opposition between the individual and the state – the opposition that would define the spiritual climate in the country for a long time to come. Those who were known as "liberal intelligentsia" held on to their conscience, defending banned manuscripts and trying to unshelve the shelved films, signing petitions and protesting on Red Square. We should recognize and do justice to each and every one of them. And not only them, but also those who helped with money and work, who risked their careers publishing and distributing the dissidents' work, who gave them shelter or just a cup of tea. Those who encouraged the protests and even those who did not discourage them. We should praise them all as they confirmed but one idea: that an individual is above the state. This was the strongest blow to the utopia ever.

Let us be fair to the years of stagnation. Of course, that period was a dead, mummified, stifled Present without a beginning and an end, with no Past or Future. But hard spiritual work continued almost invisibly. And if we compare the destiny of *Ilyich Square* with that of Andrei Tarkovsy's *Mirror* (1975), Brezhnev's "stagnation" would seem even more attractive than the Khrushchev's "thaw." Tarkovsy, just like Khutsiev, was ostracized, but without hysteria, without the party jargon, without shamanic incantations about patriotism. *The Mirror* was sentenced quietly and routinely, almost as if the judges were ashamed of themselves, almost as if they, too, knew that an individual was above the state.

This belief would sneak in and influence our culture in the worst years of stagnation when nothing, it seemed, could sneak in and all influences were forbidden. In cinema, it expressed itself, unexpectedly, in such a box office smash as *Moscow Does Not Believe in Tears* (1979), written by Valentin Chernykh and directed by Vladimir Menshov.

*Moscow Does Not Believe in Tears* openly celebrated what Grigori Alexandrov's *Spring* (1946) only dared to suggest – the dream of family life. Drawing from Hollywood Cinderella formula, this Oscar-winning movie unequivocally offered a recipe for success that anyone could use. The characters one identified with were typical of the "stagnation" period: a female general manager and a blue-collar worker. Self-made individuals, they managed their destinies as if the state were not a part of it at all. They built their own paradise, with fancy bathrooms and white telephones. Thus, the "salon" style, against which the "sixtiesniks" struggled so hard, won a triumphant victory in *Moscow Does Not Believe in Tears.*

Far from dissident free-thinking, Chernykh and Menshov simply sensed what was in the air at the time. However, individualism was not the only pressure on collective subconscious. Next to the Stalinist, there was no period in Russian history as deprived of true spirituality and as filled with pseudospiritual rhetoric as the Brezhnev period.

The rhetoric was not so senseless. "Spirituality" turned out to be the last mask behind that the agonizing utopia was hiding. And it tempted the most worthy and wise. They would beat an individual with the club of "spirituality" for expressing natural pragmatism, which they called "greedy materialism." These were the metastases of the utopia that had no more power to scare people or even to make them laugh. Individualists had only to wait a bit longer for their hour to come.

After a few years, that hour arrived. Ironically, no one else but the "sixtiesniks" made it possible. Having declared that "an individual is above the state," they performed a bitter parabola and began to defend the philistines, still alien to them, as quixotically as they had once slapped them. In fact, today, they are the only ones who care for the philistines. In my evasive and languid, cynical and estranged generation, there is none of that unselfishness, devotion to an ideal, and especially, readiness to defend others.

So let us bless the last romantics for their last blessing to us.

# Jobless prophets: Glasnost and the auteurs

*Lev Karakhan*

In the universal tug-of-war between art and commerce, Soviet cinema has always sided with the former. This contemplative streak runs deep in Russian literature, and its origins long precede the advent of cinematography. It is then no surprise that foreign films – Indian, Egyptian, French, American, and so on – top the lists of box office hits. There have been Soviet blockbusters, too, such as the 1980 Oscar-winning *Moscow Does Not Believe in Tears* (1979), which sold 90 million tickets at home. But its director, Vladimir Menshov, would certainly refuse to allow it to be pigeonholed as a purely commercial film. On the contrary, Menshov saw his version of a Soviet Cinderella as a personal revelation.

The only faithful servant of the box office is director Stanislav Govorukhin, acclaimed for his gangster miniseries *The Meeting Place Cannot Be Changed* (1979). With enviable zeal, and considerable risk to his reputation, he advocates "low cinema" rather than the high-brow film *auteur*.

To be a film maker in a country with cultural as well as political totalitarianism has always meant to be an artist; being an artist has been compared to being a prophet; and being a prophet led one straight to martyrdom. Attempts have been made to simulate martyrdom, as it alone seemed to provide admission to the ranks of the immortals. Financial success, on the contrary, has always connoted mediocrity here. Even a popular director like Nikita Mikhalkov (*Dark Eyes* [1987], *Close to Eden* [1992]), whose films were nonpolitical and stylized, has long downplayed his success by claiming to be in constant confrontation with the cinema *apparatchiks*.

But times have changed. *Perestroika* gave artists a reprieve from the tireless guardianship of the state. It also relieved them from the commitment to opposition and to the prophet's burden. Revelations became the business not of free-thinking *auteurs* but of politicians, economists, historians, and journalists.

These changes have consequently affected Russian film auteur. Its structure was created in the 1960s and 1970s by such film makers as Andrei Tarkovsky, the philosopher and spiritual healer; Vasily Shukshin, the chronicler of rural life; Gleb Panfilov, the social analyst; Sergei Paradjanov,

**30**

the master of cinematic ornamentation; Otar Ioseliani, the connoisseur of human failings; and Ilya Averbakh, the champion of Russian intelligentsia. Today, such intellectual cinema is nowhere to be found. And suffering most are the film makers who, having failed as prophets, now find themselves jobless.

Roman Balayan, the director of the celebrated *Flights at Night and in Daydreams* (1983), a brilliant study of an outcast mentality, today makes films that have no connection to the present. His films are talked about rather by inertia or out of respect for his past success. For years, there has been no word from another preperestroika darling, Alexei German, whose exceptional stories about ordinary people living in the grip of Stalinism (*Trial on the Road* [1979/1986], *Twenty Days Without War* [1978], and *My Friend Ivan Lapshin* [1984]) first revealed the tragedy of the 1930s–1940s.

Auteurs have lost their privilege of opposition, so what is left for them to hold on to? The various attempts of several film makers to survive under new circumstances outline some of the prospects.

Director Kira Muratova has taken a bolder stand than the others. Her early free-thinking pictures, *Brief Encounters* (1968) and *Long Farewell* (1971), colored with pessimism in the face of imminent political crackdown, were shelved for years. She was harassed and urged to quit directing. Her comeback feature, *Twist of Fate* (1987), based upon the Somerset Maugham story, *The Letter*, avoided any direct social implications. It spelled out her newfound distrust in "messages" and faith in "film for film's sake." In exquisite detail, it dissected the psychoanatomy of a woman (played in William Wyler's *The Letter* by Bette Davis) who murdered her lover.

Sergei Paradjanov, once a visionary of "poetic cinema," also remained aloof from political turmoil. Since returning from the Brezhnev prison camps Paradjanov, who died in 1990, made two features: *The Legend of the Suram Fortress* (1984) and *Ashik Kerib* (1988). As both films proved, the art of ancient Central Asian miniature painting was for this maverick film maker more important than all the cataclysms of the world.

The young but accomplished Ivan Dykhovichny is similarly obsessed with visual perfection. Bound by the pictorial beauty of Tarkovsky's films, Dykhovichny achieved spectacular results in lighting and detail in his 1988 production of Chekhov's *Black Monk* (1988), filmed by former Tarkovsky's cameraman Vadim Yusov. Although *The Black Monk* received a special prize for visuals at the Venice film festival, Dykhovichny could hardly be called an original artist. A smart and capable imitator, he is not a commander of style but rather its slave, tense and dependent on Tarkovsky's legacy.

Sergei Solovyev, free of any internal restraint and addictive influence, is more proficient in his exercises in style. He made his name in the years of "stagnation" as a part of the second, not so liberal, and not so nonconformist generation of the postwar film auteur. In his 1986 film *The Wild Pigeon*, a story of young pigeon keepers set in the 1950s, he concocted a spicy cocktail of treacle and kerosene by blending the romantic caprice, juvenile sensuality and extremism of his earlier films with Alexei German's austere "slum" baroque. In *Assa* (1987), Solovyev burst onto the youth rock scene. His last perestroika picture *Black Rose Stands for Sorrow, Red Rose Stands for Love* (1989) was a resolute attempt to mainstream what he calls the genre of "decay" or the decadent methods of the underground "parallel cinema."*

On the other hand, "parallel" film makers attempts to gain legitimacy in the mainstream, such as the Aleinikov brothers' 1989 Mosfilm production *Somebody Was Here*, failed. What was funny and charming in "samizdat," on 16 mm, with no budget and with friends serving as actors, crew, and audience, turned artless and pretentious on the professional screen.

Still, one independent picture penetrated the mainstream with all its underground qualities – dark, dissonant images; noncontinuity editing; exposed gimmicks and techniques – intact. *The Name Day* was shot by Sergei Selyanov and Nikolai Makarov at an amateur studio in the small Russian town of Tula in the early 1980s and released nationally in 1988. Compressing various periods of Soviet history into one, *The Name Day* discusses, through its teenage hero, the rationality of the ethics of our past and present.

*The Name Day*, though alternative and experimental, still advocates the artistic mission, canonized by Alexander Pushkin as "to scorch with words the hearts of men." Not one of the Soviet auteurs could renounce it outright, no matter how far away they departed from it in their stylistic search; not even the diehard "renegades" like Sergei Solovyev, who was the first to sacrifice intellectualism to commercialism and exchange art goods for hard currency. So what if the idea sprang from the greed that accompanied the new market freedom and not from aesthetic conviction, typical of current film auteur in the West.

As the standard film industry infrastructures are missing here, Solovyev himself serves, not without talent and passion, as an agent, a public relations person and a producer. He is not alone. Director Alexander Kaidanovsky, whom Solovyev regards as an ally, is far less energetic, but no less market-oriented, as his 1988 film *The Kerosene Seller's Wife* (1989) demonstrates. From philosophical adaptations of the short stories by Jorge Luis Borges (*The Garden* [1984] and *The Guest* [1988]) and Leo Tolstoy (*The Simple Death* [1985]) in the early 1980s, Kaidanovsky moved on to a sus-

---

*See the related essay by Sergei Dobrotvorsky in this volume, "The Most Avant-Garde of All Parallel Ones." – Eds.

penseful postwar detective story that irritates the viewer's subconscious and does not reveal its true intention.

Kaidanovsky belongs to the new generation of film makers for whom to sit "between the two chairs" of the box office and elitist tastes is neither unnatural nor uncomfortable. Moreover, this generation's "in-between" attitude dictates its artistic idiom. This is especially true of the "Leningrad film school." In *Mr. Decorator* (1987), which utilizes the turn-of-the-century "Art Nouveau" style, Oleg Teptsov produced an arty thriller about a murderous fashion mannequin. Valery Ogorodnikov, who devoted his first feature, *The Burglar* (1987), to the reckless heavy-metal generation, attempted a more bizarre and resourceful, if not altogether successful, historical spectacle about the Stalinist legacy in *Prishvin's Paper Eyes* (1989). Konstantin Lopushansky, who developed the genre of futuristic film disaster, confronts the viewer with nuclear holocaust (*Letters from a Dead Man* [1987]) and ecological apocalypse (*Visitor to a Museum* [1989]).

Unlike Lopushansky, who does "flash-forwards," Sergei Ovcharov prefers flashbacks. Using the visual code of the "naive" folk art, he reminds us of the flagrant contradictions of the Russian national character in films such as *The Left-Hander* (1988) and *It* (1989).

Strange as it may be, the cinema of prophetic experiment is best represented today by those who despise didactic preaching. Take the Kazakh "new wave," inaugurated by Rashid Nugmanov with his first feature, *The Needle* (1988). A story of drugs and rock 'n' roll, *The Needle* endorses, if somewhat mockingly, romanticism and unmasks the bankruptcy of the old social values.

So does Vasily Pichul's striking *Little Vera* (1988), which traces the mishaps of a provincial Soviet family. Little Vera's passionate desire to believe in something amid the ruins of the social system (and not the erotic scene that shook up the Soviets) was what kept the audiences spellbound. Largely due to its simplicity and straightforward naturalism, *Little Vera* became a sensational box-office smash, attracting fifty million viewers in its first year, the year of generally declining interest in film. Since glasnost, only Georgian film auteurs have eschewed participation in the division of the commercial film pie. Time has altered their artistic horizons, but not their ethical stand of independence and responsibility. During the years of stagnation, Georgian film makers often looked back at the folkloric past to support human dignity and values. After glasnost, they began to research the consequences of the moral genocide that shattered Soviet society.

Alexander Tsabadze's *Spot* (1985) and Vakhtang Kotetishvili's *Anemia* (1988) focus on the young men, restless and lost. Levan Tutberidze's *Nazar's Last Prayer* (1988), which shows the execution of the Georgian Metropolitan by the communists, projects the crimes of the first years of the Soviet power onto the present.

Yet, the young film makers have a long way to go to reach the height to which the Georgian film has been brought by Alexander Rekhviashvili. Throughout the 1980s, Rekhviashvili was permitted to have the last word on our youth (in *The Step*) and on our recent history (in *The Georgian Chronicle of the 19th Century* [1979] and *The Way Home* [1982]). But like many others, he remained silent throughout glasnost,* while the young were learning to analyze reality without any reference to an ultimate truth.

Prophets were forced to reevaluate their goals. Perhaps only Vadim Abdrashitov is still loyal to message films as if nothing has changed. Abdrashitov made a name at home and abroad with his socially poignant dramas *The Defense's Summing-up* (1976), *The Turn* (1978), *The Fox Hunt* (1980), *The Train Has Stopped* (1982), *The Planet Parade* (1984), and *Plumbum* (1987). In *The Manservant* (1989), a glasnost parable of the strange relationship between a high-ranking *apparatchik* and his chauffeur, Abdrashitov attempted to introduce more stylistic subtlety than usual, but he failed, unable to overcome his straightforward and judgmental instincts.

Finally, a few thoughts about the best known and the most controversial Soviet auteur – Alexander Sokurov. His underground *Man's Lonely Voice* (1978/87), based on Andrei Platonov's prose and made during the stagnation years, was an artistic breakthrough that linked the names of Sokurov and Tarkovsky. Sokurov evidently aspired to succeed the Master as the leader of Soviet intellectual film. And so he did after Tarkovsky's emigration and death, which preceded the unshelving of Sokurov's films by the new free-thinking administration. In actuality, however, Tarkovsky's throne remains vacant despite all of Sokurov's prophetical aspirations for he is a different kind of leader. Filming feverishly and in confusion, sometimes several films (both features and documentaries) a year, Sokurov may be likened to Wim Wenders rather than to Tarkovsky, who made only seven films in his lifetime. Among Sokurov's numerous productions (some say 20) only a few have genuine artistic merit, such as *The Evening Sacrifice*, a 1984 documentary about a Victory Day parade in Leningrad, and the apocalyptic *Days of Eclipse* (1988). Nonetheless, Sokurov's impact derives from the totality of his films, which possess a sort of cinematic hypnotism that exerts an almost mystical control over the viewer's consciousness.

This transcendental power over the human spirit is perhaps the only property left to our prophets by these new circumstances in which people's physical health is handled by television healers. But in such delicate matters who can tell a clairvoyant from a charlatan.

---

*This essay was written before Rekhviashvili's next film, *Coming Closer*, was released in 1991, thus marking, ironically, the end of glasnost along with the end of the film maker's silence. – Eds.

# Midseasonal anarchists: Youth consciousness and youth culture in the cinema of perestroika

*Marina Drozdova*

Russia, a country with a continental climate, is notorious for its tendency to go to extremes. It pays a high price for it, too.

Have not we paid dearly for the "great illusion" of the concept of "socialism in one country?" This is the way it goes: overbearing, merciless freeze in the wintertime and overwhelming heat in the summer. In midseasons, a considerable number of citizens – compliant fatalists – become irritated. They prefer either heat or cold to the autumn slush.

But the times of the Brezhnevist stagnation have given birth to a generation of "midseasonal" people who are unequivocally inspired by the mild European climate and quietly envy the comfort it has to offer. These people are the older part of the so-called young generation, and, hence, the creators of one of this generation's cultural strata.

The younger part, roughly fifteen to twenty-two years of age, whose adolescence and youth are influenced by the winds of change, are closer to anarchists. Seasons bother them as much as anything else happening within the national borders.

It is difficult to define all the composite features of progressive youth culture. During the years of stagnation, we believed it to include everything beyond the slogan "the people and the party are one." At the time, very few people were expecting freedom. And yet, here it is. Or, rather, it has been proclaimed. The state started stripping itself of ideological officiality. But it did so in a very peculiar manner – exposing the most unexpected parts of itself at the most unexpected moments, acting with the passion of a hot lover one instant and with the modesty and unwillingness of a virgin the next.

Everything became confused. The system began to converge with the former underground, which since has lost its prefix *under*. Midseasonal domestic don't-give-a-damners never get too enthusiastic about the state of things. Their position of outsiders is represented in the cinema of the past four years by the postmodern mode. With its aesthetic quotations and manner of acting, postmodernism provides a new language for speaking about old themes.

The films of this artistic trend – Rashid Nugmanov's *The Needle* (1988),

35

Alexander Baranov's and Bakhyt Kilibayev's *The Three* (1988), Abai Karpykov's *Little Fish In Love* (1989) – display their creators' distrust of leg-
islative power. Each of them presents his own version of a modern
character. One is a romantic dealer; the second is a social outcast true to
the theory of "small deeds," once so popular in Russia (see Anton Chekhov); the third is a tramp. All of them, however, are outcasts; none wants
to have anything to do with official ideology, even at the time when the
latter decided to shift its positions.

*Little Fish In Love* seems to be a paraphrased version of *Rumble Fish*
(1983), although director Abai Karpykov insists he has not seen the Francis
Ford Coppola movie. The main character is a young man about twenty-
five. In one scene, he finds himself looking through the glass of a home
aquarium at totally self-absorbed and complacent fish. This image is an
exact quotation from Coppola. But whereas the scene becomes a point of
intersection for the heroes of the two films, they are on opposite sides of
the triangle *man–illusion–society*.

Coppola's character is a fighter, though an abstract one. Karpykov's
character is seriously tuned in to fishlike coolness. The former offers himself and his charges to society, even if the chances that those charges will
be accepted are quite slim. The latter stays away from society: He believes
it useless to talk to a deaf ear. He never displays vain anxiety, following
the advice of Jesus of Nazareth, who did not approve of vanity that manifests our lack of faith. Plainly, Kaprykov's is an existentialist character.

So are the three drunk leads of *The Three* (1988). The social group to
which they belong is described by the term "BOMZH" (Russian abbrevi-
ation for "Without a Definite Place of Residence"). Drunk as skunks with
cheap booze, the three pals sign up to perform a risky stunt for a visiting
film crew. (What the hell for? Oh, mysterious Russian soul!) The fee they
earn is thrown to the winds. They do not need money; money is not a
value for them. They just have fun, and then they split.

This is another fully existentialist story; its subject is "life in general,
life itself, life and nothing but." "In general" is one of our favorite expressions, symbolizing the sweetest uncertainty. "In general" is the static
version of "maybe." It deals with life beyond any rules, beyond the struggle for or against them, beyond unavoidable ways and circumstances.

Unfortunately, this playful direction looks all too pale next to the thick
mainstream that tends to concentrate on most serious social problems.

One of the first films to deal with this formerly forbidden topic is a
feature documentary, *Confession: The Chronicle of Alienation* (1988), directed by Georgy Gavrilov.

The picture, a confession of a thirty-year-old drug addict, grandson of
a warden in a state labor camp, was shot over a period of several years and
graphically depicted the user's descent into complete doom and hopelessness. This was one of the first gains of the ideological independence

granted to the artists – the possibility of showing fatal predestination of somebody or something.

The confessor attempts to rid himself of his deadly habit in a prisonlike drug clinic. Unsuccessfully, he tries to find a job and create a family. His underage wife also becomes a user, unable to give up drugs even during her pregnancy or after giving birth.

The hero's attitude and life-style vividly exemplify supreme don't-give-a-damnism. An approximate parallel to it could be found in Paul Morissey's masterpiece *Trash* (1970), which investigated the totally decayed and worn-out consciousness of an American anarchist in the late 1960s. Despite the artistic differences the parallel is clear: Spiritual rebellion in a totalitarian society is being detached and devaluated by the machine; it is shielded from public attention by *Pravda* editorials and such.

It may seem that I refer only to the past. But personal time usually lags behind, and today, we find ourselves to be disciples of Marcel Proust. As we make our past public, it becomes a much more actual reality than the present. In years past, who could possibly have thought of such a close kinship between the aristocrat Proust and the offspring of Bolshevism?

Even if dissidence has faded into the past, youth culture still depends on the dissident attitude and life-style. Artists know better than anyone else: The past can revive at any moment.

Dissidence is the destiny of people who do not see life as a game. Or, at least, they determine their place in the rules of the game very firmly. And they pay a high price for allowing themselves to be "real." Unlike the "useless people" typical of Russia, these are active individuals.

This is how the lead of Valery Zheregi's *Dissident* (1989) is presented to us. He is a thirty-something writer who exhausts himself with reflections on the ideological pressure blocking his creativity. At the same time, he works at a radio station, jamming broadcasts of the Western "free" voices. He goes on a trip to Europe and there shoots a video about his homeland. But the picture seems fake to him, so he makes another version of it back home.

As in that video, everything in *Dissident* itself is fake, including its style and its hero. Film critic Alexander Kiselev wrote that the protagonist's standpoint is based on denial, which, Kiselev points out, paradoxically brings our sweet dissident into a peculiar group of pathologically loyal citizens displeased with absolutely everything. Take away the power of official dogma and his perspective will instantaneously fall apart. He wants to be a "dissident" just to be something. But neither he nor the director will acknowledge it. Both display a classically distorted mentality, tortured by ideological wickedness – a moral color blindness. This most frightening feature of the young generation leads to devaluation of everything and everyone.

For the young people of the 1970s and 1980s, rock music has become a kind of moral code. *Rock* (1988), a feature documentary directed by Alexei Uchitel, is devoted to the Soviet rock legends, illegal for almost a decade. Boris Grebenshchikov, Victor Tsoi, Yuri Shevchuk – they all speak for their generation. In the picture, they talk about themselves, their friends, and share their ideas of the state and power.

In the 1970s, Soviet rock music was rather chamber, especially in comparison to Western standard. The so-called new wave of Soviet rock 'n' roll that derived from the "old wave" but emerged in the times of glasnost (that is, legality) gave its microphones to the new type of young angry men. The films about them – *The Arsonists* (1989), *The Burglar* (1987), *Tragedy in Rock* (1988), *The Blackmailer* (1988), *The Homunculus* (1989) – picture a sinister crowd. These and other films with less brutal and spectacular titles fill the screens with images of teenage anarchy. Unlike the films we have already discussed, these do not deal with youth culture and consciousness on the levels of style and atmosphere. They contain attempts at semisociological research, recorded in a traditional mode (yet beyond the strict orientation of socialist realism, proclaimed dead by the sixth congress of the Film Makers' Union, as if this aesthetic phantom was ever alive). One way or another, the film makers try to use youth images – pop and rock music and iconography – which results in nothing but the effect of mechanical copying.

The cameras focus on young boys and girls offended by society and not trying to hide their pain. The movies show them at school and with their families, friends, and lovers. They envy and betray, sometimes they are dressed to kill, sometimes they fight their demons. Nothing inspires them except the concepts of absolute freedom and absolute power. This reflects a stunning phenomenon: For almost a century, the citizens of this society of supposed equal rights and opportunities have been searching for ways to secure at least some individual rights. The result is an aggressive nihilism.

The recent film nihilists resemble Bazarov, the classical late-nineteenth-century nihilist from Ivan Turgenev's novel, *Fathers and Sons*. But the modern nihilists do not belong to the aristocracy as Bazarov did. Unlike the early nihilists, who rejected the existing conditions by way of conscience, the new nihilists are simply irritated with social inconveniences.

This idea is expressed in *The Husband and Daughter of Tamara Alexandrovna* (1989), written by Nadezhda Kozhushannaya and directed by Olga Narutskaya, a story of the mental and physical decay of a young father and his thirteen-year-old daughter. The picture is made in a style untraditional for the Soviet screen: the aesthetics of ugliness. The hopeless shabbiness of everyday life is the leading character of the film. The conclusion it prompts is that in such conditions humanity simply switches itself off.

At least two possible conclusions to my survey should be made. First and foremost, the new radical attitude has found its more or less accurate reflection on the screen. That is exactly where our future lies. Regrettably, however, the punk style that flourished here in the atmosphere of perestroika (having appeared in this country under the influence of postpunk trends in Western art) is fading away.

The second conclusion is that one group of the young generation has not yet found its reflection on the screen. These are our yuppies, young businessmen, the nouveaux riches who have no self-doubts. Patriarchal late-nineteenth-century Russia regarded such people as a threat to the spirit. How will Russia of the late twentieth-century accept them? I doubt that the process will be entirely painless. We continue to search for our directions. The question put by Nikolai Gogol 150 years ago renews itself sharply today: "Where are you heading to, Russia?"

# The most avant-garde of all parallel ones: The times and ways of the Soviet independents

*Sergei Dobrotvorsky*

Before the mid-1980s, it was hard to believe that parallel (or independent, alternative, or underground) cinema was possible in the Soviet Union at all. Other forms of artistic expression here learned how to trick the taboos. Secluded corners of the "underground" could always accommodate a typewriter or an easel. Rock 'n' roll rebels could always utilize a set of second-hand instruments and a mono cassette player to the utmost pleasure of their groupies and to the great confusion of the Western producers, who vainly attempted to turn the quantity of Russian rock legends into the quality of sound.

The secret life of film could not be so easy. Film, however inexpensive, remains a sum of technologies and a social product. And yet free cinema exists. Shot modestly on 8-mm or 16-mm film, sometimes on video, and rarely on professional 35-mm, it has its own authorities and connoisseurs, festivals and a magazine, *Cine-Phantom*, published privately in Moscow. It also has two independent branches, in Moscow and Leningrad, that coexist in mutual respect despite their opposing viewpoints.

Muscovites are easier to write about, if only because ideas of conceptualism are firmly rooted in Moscow cultural history. Concept comes from a word and turns into a word. Unlike the self-conscious Muscovites, the Leningradians refrain from theorizing. They prefer murky aphorisms and made-up authorities.

Usually, independence in art is associated with the avant-garde. In the past, our critics, nauseated by any art that was out of norm, would label it with an "-ism." We must now clarify the terms. Whereas avant-garde is an aesthetic concept, independence is a social phenomenon. Avant-garde is self-sufficient; but the "parallel" inevitably requires another line. Strictly speaking, our avant-garde is all in Moscow, whereas "parallel cinema" belongs to Leningrad. Muscovites focus on pure expressiveness, experimenting with form, searching for new frontiers of the art language. Leningradians are more interested in inventing a shock therapy for social consciousness. The Moscow school could appear under any social circumstances, but not the Leningrad. The Moscow films are more exciting to discuss than to watch. The Leningrad films are more obscure, but also more entertaining.

The leaders of the Moscow school are the brothers Igor and Gleb Aleinikov. Their works combine *cinema direct*, conceptualism, and meditation with the elements of "soc-art." Add conflicting visual textures (often shooting from the TV screen, the Aleinikovs mix fiction with documentary footage) and whimsical editing, and you will have a movie that reaches completion only before the audience. Cinematic speech here develops into a special case of language – each sign becomes a prototype for the whole; each text turns into its own context.

The Aleinikovs' case proves how incidental the relationship is between the avant-garde and society, even as rigid a society as the Soviet one. The film makers see all social concepts as if they were reflected in Lewis Carroll's *Looking Glass*. These concepts are nothing to them but the items of mass mythology or a set of stereotypes. The Aleinikovs' *Tractors* (1987), for example, is an out-of-synch reexamination of the myth of the "iron horse"; for them, traditional communist values are just a pretext for playful meditation.

The Leningrad underground film co-op, Mja-la-la-film, was founded by Yevgeny Yufit, Andrei "the Dead" Kurmoyartsev, Yevgeny "the Idiot" Kondratyev, Oleg Kotelnikov, and Denis Kuzmin. Soon, they were joined by Konstantin Mitenev, Igor Bezrukov, Andrei Medvedev, Ivan Sotnikov, Georgy Malyshev, Inal Savchenko, Sergei Vinokurov, and Ivetta Pomerantseva.

Yevgeny Yufit tells a story of how the police confiscated one of the first reels shot by the members of Mja-la-la-film; it contained a sequence of wrestling in a garbage heap. Soon the film was returned with the verdict that it was too idiotic to be considered law breaking. One must give credit to the keen insight of the Leningrad police who guessed the main principle of the Leningrad school long before it came onto the art critics' horizon. The aesthetic attitude of the Leningradians (they often call themselves the "new cinema" to manifest their kinship with the "new" painting and music) is in repudiating sense altogether, raising absurdity to an absolute degree.

The characters in the Leningrad pictures resemble molecules, seen through a microscope, as they endlessly race, intersect, and collide. They are wretched monsters, phantoms of the "communal apartments" and city dumps. They are mongrels and degenerates, necrophiliacs and corpses (not to be confused with commercial cinema's zombies).

Despite all its chaos, the Leningrad school does not abandon traditional film structures, coherent plot, and characters. But every structure here is turned inside out: The pursued chases the pursuer and a character whom we thought we knew acts quite opposite to what is expected of him. In

Yevgeny Yufit's instant classic, *The Orderly Werewolves* (1985), a gang of white-gowned nurses butcher a patient. In *Lumberjack* (1985), an engineer stops the train half a meter in front of a man laying on the tracks, only to kick him to death. In *Spring* (1987), a man escapes pursuers only to commit suicide by smashing his head against a tree.

It is idiotic indeed. But idiocy is essential for dealing with the distorted world the Leningrad film makers see. With integrity that distinguishes art from fraud, the "new" Leningradians depict the world as a totalitarian system that, having lost every bit of sense, still has all the means of control and oppression.

It is easy to attribute the new cinema to the times of Brezhnevist stagnation. According to this relevant, if banal, interpretation, the young film makers criticize and protest within the limits of the historical situation. But the global community of the pop culture era does not fit into any state limits.

The Russian dissidents of the 1950s and 1960s did not go beyond traditional ideological boundaries. The assumption that any ideology works on oppression came later, in the 1970s. This can be seen by comparing the lyrics of the folk songs of the 1950s through 1970s and the rock 'n' roll texts of the 1980s. Even the most radical criticism of the former is based upon social ethics, whereas the rock culture is searching for a substance apart from all laws or regulations, however liberal they might be.

The result is liberation from the political and other taboos. In *The Post-Political Cinema* (1988), the Aleinikov brothers splice together portraits of Lenin and Eisenstein. Yevgeny Kondratyev builds his little masterpiece, *Idiot Am I to Forget* . . . (1986), on repetition of one simple act: walking in the snow. Long ago, Eisenstein created the "vertical montage" – a composite ideology that emerges from the connection of visual motions. Today, Kondratyev speaks of the "vertical cinema," making a reverse move toward decomposed ideology and meaningless image.

Totalitarianism always causes violence. Yevgeny Yufit, the leader of one of the new cinema's main branches, "necrorealism," knows this well. His short and elaborate tales are full of morgues and funerals, postmortem clowning and suicidal grotesquery. He claims that among his influences are Bunuel, the French avant-garde film makers of the 1920s, and Edward Von Hoffman – a pathologist who wrote an extensive study of forensics.

Yufit's corpses have nothing in common with the monsters of horror films. Their screen life, accentuated by fast motion and abrupt editing, recalls Mack Sennett rather than George Romero. But in contrast with the classical slapstick comedy, masters of which considered motion to be this century's dominant force and adopted violence only as a spectacle for the victory of the human spirit, action in Yufit's films is not only illogical but also totally aimless.

The Leningrad "parallel" scene, however, is not confined to necrorealist search. For example, Oleg Kotelnikov, a professional painter, cultivates one of the various animation techniques appropriated by the new artists. Producing his short subjects right before showing them, Kotelnikov draws every frame by scratching the film emulsion. This method, which turns each copy into an individual act of art, was first used in the 1920s by Viking Eggeling and Walter Ruttmann, and later by the New York underground cinema.

The new openness, having terminated the state monopoly in film, altered the idea of nonconformity. It also helped to spread information and made it possible for various styles and genres to interact.

Just as "parallel" movies have penetrated, though uncredited, mainstream productions, such as Sergei Solovyev's *Assa* (1987) and Alexander Sokurov's *Days of Eclipse* (1988), the high-brow avant-gardists Aleinikovs have penetrated the commercial film industry, thus refuting their own stand. Yevgeny Kondratyev's style, on the contrary, developed into an almost academic hermetism and virtuosity in *Daydreams* (1988) and *Fire in the Nature* (1988). In Moscow, Pyotr Pospelov explores a poetic documentary genre, whereas Boris Yukhananov champions energetic "video-karate," which for him means shooting without a camera. In Leningrad, the Che-payev film group (named after an imaginary mutant between Che-Gevara and Vasily Chapayev, the Russian Civil War hero who went on to become a classical movie character and a national myth) claimed its task to be "improvement of reality by means of total cinema." The poet Alexei Feoktistov expressed his postindustrial visions in *Battle for a Fleet* (1989), the footage of which he did not direct but mysteriously found at the fire exit of his house.

Other centers have joined Moscow and Leningrad in their "parallel" march. In Riga, Lvov, Minsk, and elsewhere, the new cinema slowly but surely fosters a new audience, overcoming distrust and traditional inertia. In search of purity and integrity, it is daring to reimplant the once cutoff branch of the Russian avant-garde onto the main trunk of World Culture.

1989

## Postscript

"Life after death is really swell, pals!"

This line from the hymn of the necrorealists could be an epigraph to the current state of things in Soviet "parallel film" – or, rather, formerly

Soviet and formerly parallel. Death of ideology, once called upon with such passion by the monsters of film underground, finally had arrived. The former "parallel" geometry of cultural independence disappeared with this arrival. The parallels crossed and got mixed up in the new social space.

For the majority of film makers, the situation presented a choice: to go above the surface or to sink deeper into the subcultural grounds. Each of them solved this problem in his own way. Having played out their leadership in "parallel film," the Aleinikov brothers became Mosfilm directors, with two medium-length films, *Somebody Was Here* (1989) and *Waiting for DeBill* (1991), as well as a feature, *The Tractor Drivers* (1992), a remake of the classic Stalinist comedy, in their file.

In St. Petersburg, Maxim Pezhemsky, who in the recent past was a member of the Che-payev film group, made *Comrade Chkalov's Crossing of the North Pole* (1989). The film reinterprets by reediting the official film biographies of Chkalov, the famous aviator of the 1930s, in the manner that marries Mack Sennett's slapstick with Georges Méliès's fantasy.

Necrorealism, which for several years substituted in this country for horror genre, has developed into film auteur, becoming "a scary black-and-white film" in the style of a young David Lynch. Having grown up and grown, necrorealists now realize their screen experiments within the St. Petersburg film studio, Lenfilm. There Yevgeny Yufit conceived his first 35-mm works, *The Knights of Heaven* (1989) and *Daddy, Santa Claus Is Dead* (1992). Extravagant and slow, they look as if Robert Bresson, having just seen *Night of the Living Dead* (1968), stood behind the camera. They also remind us more of a tired culture of the end of this millennium than a bold avant-garde of the recent past. All that remains unchanged is Yufit and Company's black humor. Not coincidentally, *Daddy, Santa Claus Is Dead* won the first prize at the festival in Rimini, Fellini's birthplace.

Among those who preferred the underground freedom to the temptation of the mainstream film industry, Yevgeny Kondratyev is the most notable. Working as an actor in the Aleinikov brothers' films, he also continues his own directing experiments in what he calls "incorrect cinema." As always, one can catch those little masterpieces only in the dirty garrets or basements, projected on the wall. Somewhere in the elite *tusovka*, the voice of Boris Yukhananov, formerly a self-proclaimed magician of free video art, slowly fades out. The Leningrad *videoaste* Vadim Drapkin resides in Israel, although every day there is someone who says they just saw him on Nevsky Prospect. Reportedly, Pyotr Pospelov, director of a charming parallel feature *The Report From the Land of Love* (1988), returns more and more often to his first profession of musicologist.

The others do what they can. In the current deideologized state of affairs, any idea can pass, even one that a few years ago would have led you into an institution. But as the whole country now looks like a madhouse, there is no place to go and no reason to be put away.

So after all, life after death is really swell!

1993

# PART TWO

# Glasnost's top ten°

# CHAPTER I
# Repentance

The film's narrative concerns three generations in an imaginary city ruled by a tyrant, Varlam Aravidze, whose name in Georgian means "nobody" and who dies early in the film. Repeated efforts to bury and keep buried the tyrant's large body prove fruitless, and this simple plot device becomes an allegory for horrors committed against the people by Stalin, Hitler, and other autocrats.

*Repentance* (*Pokayaniye*), directed by Tengiz Abuladze; screenplay by Nana Djanelidze, Tengiz Abuladze, and Rezo Kveselava; cinematography by Mikhail Agranovich; production design by Georgi Mikeladze; music compiled by Nana Djanelidze. Cast: Avtandil Makharadze (Varlam Aravidze, Abel Aravidze), Ia Ninidze, Merab Ninidze, Zeinab Botsvadze, Ketevan Abuladze, Edisher Giorgobiani, and Kahi Kavsadze. Color, 155 min. Gruzia-film Studios production, 1984.

1. The Middle Ages meet the present when totalitarianism is on trial in Tengiz Abuladze's richly textured, but one-dimensionally allegorical, preglasnost satire *Repentance* (1984). (Photo: Kinocenter and Sovexportfilm.)

# On the road that leads to the truth

*Tatyana Khloplyankina*

The release of *Repentance* (1984) is one of those big events that certify that the order of our life is happily and inevitably changing.

Only yesterday such a picture would have seemed impossible. Working on it was an act of personal courage for director Tengiz Abuladze, his co-writers, Nana Djanelidze and Rezo Kveselava, and those leaders of the Georgian film industry who greenlighted the project.

Today the film is out. Our task is to decipher it aptly. But here is the unexpected rub.

*Repentance* is a truly philosophical work, complex and difficult, as it speaks to us in the language of metaphors and symbols, mixing up reality and imagination as well as epochs, costumes, and styles. One should examine every frame of it, explain why contemporary details meet medieval trivia, and thoroughly analyze it both in a philosophical and cinematic context. But at the same time, one realizes that any attempt to penetrate the film with an analytical scalpel would be impossible, almost criminal today. When a hungry person receives a loaf of bread, this person does not want to or cannot examine the baker. When a thirsty person sees a spring, this person clings to it without thinking about what this liquid consists of.

*Repentance* satisfies our tremendous thirst for truth and our urge to reevaluate the mistakes of the recent past. It is indeed a work of art. But first of all it is a fact of our current social life.

It would be easy to avoid comparing the film with our history. The action takes place in an imaginary country. The looks of the main character – Mayor Varlam, who drowned his city in blood – do not resemble those of any particular historical figure. All in all, the film is a pure fantasy. Bodies being unburied and delivered back to their family's doorsteps (this strange event opens the picture) are unheard of. Nor does history recall dictators who in their spare time would pay visits to their vassals, sing operatic arias there, and then depart through a window, jumping straight into the saddle of a horse. Viewers, unprepared for these twists of the film maker's imagination, may be stunned at first. But then again these twists have their origins in reality.

51

Unnatural lust for acting in a theater of blood, pompous rituals, and cat-and-mousing with the victims are in the nature of any dictator, starting, perhaps, with Nero. Imaginary Mayor Varlam Aravidze took over the obsession from his real-life predecessors. Had the film makers' imagination gone totally wild, they could not reach the level of such horrific phantasmagoria of our times as Cambodia or the Chinese cultural revolution, with its outbursts of barbarism and theatrical happenings. With his arias and cheap practical jokes, Varlam would seem a choirboy against this background.

In a life of the individual, as well as in the life of a people, there are moments when reality is so horrendous that all one could say is: It can't be, it's a bad dream. *Repentance* works in the rhythm of such a nightmare. Its texture is misty, unstable, strange, and confused. We are scared, and what gives us relief is that these are somebody else's dreams, not our own. But then the moment comes when the mist dissolves and the phantasmagoria ends. All we see is a grievous line of women (future widows) and children (future orphans) waiting at the prison window. This is our own history. This is 1937.

In these prison scenes and later in the scenes at the railroad – where two women and a child are lost among the driftwood, hoping to find a mark left on the lumber by their husband, brother, and father – the direction of Tengiz Abuladze and the camerawork by Mikhail Agranovich are at their best. We see the land, naked, blackened by rains and mud; the wind is chilly. People who once lived, loved, and created beautiful art in this city have turned into chips and sawdust. They will be used, of course. Paper will be made from the chips, and portraits of the grinning scoundrel, whose spectacles remind us of Beria, will be printed on it.

Those portraits are long gone by now. But are there not people among us who cling to the past, ignoring its tragic mistakes? Is it not being heard now and then, even from young people, a horrifying surmise that under Stalin there was real order to things? But which order?

*Repentance* discharges the matter of Stalinist order with an image of the women lined up at the prison window from which a bark, not a voice, is heard. At this point, one realizes that Abuladze's film, which seemed so complicated at first, is really very simple. Its message fits in one line, but what a line that is!

At the end, the female lead, Ketevan, whose parents died in the time of repressions, clutches the newspaper with Varlam's death announcement, awakes from her memories, and comes to the window. A very old woman outside asks her, "Does this road lead to the temple?"

"No," smiles Ketevan sadly. "This is Varlam's street. It can't lead to the temple."

"Who needs a road if it does not lead to a temple?" rejoins the old lady. (Symbolically, this small but key part became an artistic testament of a great actress, Verico Andjaparidze, who died recently.) The clarity of this thought is stunning: A road that does not lead to a Temple, to Truth and Spirituality, does not lead anywhere.

Thus, the film insists on simplicity of evaluations. Good and evil are polarized and confronted. There are no characters who are simply positive; they are ideal. So the parts of artist Sandro Barateli, his wife Nino, and their daughter Ketevan are played by the incredibly handsome, spiritually luminous actors Edisher Giorgobiani, Ketevan Abuladze, and Zeinab Botsvadze. Nor are there simply bad guys: Varlam, in a gripping, courageous performance by Avtandil Makharadze, and all his men are instead repulsive. The attempts of Varlam's son Abel (also played by Makharadze) to justify his father's crimes ruin his family: As long as Varlam's body rests in peace, as long as the mistakes of the past are buried, Varlam's grandson cannot live. He kills himself, paying with his life for his father's silence and his grandfather's crimes.

It has been a while since we saw a film with such firmly determined moral standards. This morality is what makes *Repentance* so compellingly urgent. Fortunately, the past twenty years did not bring us the tragedies that the era condemned by the Twentieth Party Congress did. Yet it was a time of diluted standards. The notions of good and evil became mixed up as often happens in stagnant historical periods. Everything became conveniently "complicated." Instead of calling a villain a villain, we would shake our heads: Things are more complicated than they seem. But no, they are not! Betrayal is simple, cowardice is simple, and so are courage, honesty, beauty. So every honest person must react simply to all the changes in our country. It was glasnost that brought about urge to reveal the mistakes of the past and caused to life such a picture as *Repentance*.

One would want to watch this film endlessly. Even when all the great scenes are clearly reflected in one's mind, one would want to come back to the dark of the theater perhaps for one single shot: that of Abel, the dictator's son, digging out his father's corpse and throwing it from the hill into the sunlit crater of the city. Once is not enough. There are so many mistakes, tragedies, and lessons in the past that this scene seen once cannot satisfy our longing for vengeance and repentance. Besides, we know of too many incidents when evil, once unmasked, was declared good too soon, and the criminals' graves were redecorated with decent tombstones. That is why we would want this scene to play over and over, until everybody believes in democratic ideals.

*Repentance* is the road that leads to the Temple.

# Between the circus and the zoo

*Igor Aleinikov*

## Have you seen *Repentance*?

The light went out in the theater. On the screen, in black and white, a fat officer in an army jacket was interrogating the accused. Something morbid lit up the inspector's gaze. The interrogated man sat still as the bright desk lamp was reflected in his wide-open, somewhat clouded eyes.

The inspector locked the door and approached the accused with a smile on his quivering lips. The man kept still. The inspector pushed him down, belly on the table, and stripped off his pants. Then he turned off the bright light and began to take his victim from the rear.

The beam of a street lamp fell on the pale face of the accused. Eyes still open, the face moved along the desk, thrust by thrust. The inspector's breathing was deep and moist. He finished off his climax by stabbing the accused in the head with a pair of scissors. Yet even with scissors penetrating his skull, the victim's look did not change: He had already been dead for several days.

As you might have guessed, there is no such scene in *Repentance*. There is an inspector in a tuxedo and a white grand piano instead.

Unfortunately, the film is not even an adaptation of Solzhenitsyn. Nor is it a television miniseries with a full list of the victims and the killers of the Stalin regime. The movie turned out to be nothing of what might have been expected of it. It turned out to be nothing of a political event anyhow.

The time for aesthetic realization of the 1930s material has not yet arrived. It is necessary to say that a spade is a spade first, otherwise the historical issues will not be clear for the general audiences. This precisely is the trouble with *Repentance*.

## The art of stimulating

Actually, long before *Repentance* opened, it was clear that the movie lacked any political sex or gender. Recognizable faces, events, sharp phrases strike something in the groin, pointing at the intimacy of politics and eroticism in a society in which aerobics is considered sexual intemperance.

The film tickles most of all when it compares Stalinism to Nazism and Italian fascism. Such are the shots with the secretary–police–matron in a black-leather coat singing "Ode to Joy" in German, or the Mussoliniesque speech of Varlam; the depiction of "foreign" tortures, or even the "Moonlight Sonata" performance.

This concept is not original. I wonder what our time will be compared with in fifty years.

The most unexpected quality of *Repentance* is the perversely necrophilic tendency of this political porn. Every shot of the picture seems to be steeped in the flavor of petrification. A little more of the dance around the coffin and we shall see the corpse embrace the female, crazed by passion.

It would have been alright, even nice for some punk movie, should not the director have felt obliged to denounce the "cult of personality" and make such deep generalizations. He is guided, perhaps, by the "aesthetic" rule that is much hyped here today: "The more the better." (Generally, the new trend is quite clear. Our Soviet film art turned into a cemetery long ago, and, clearly, no flowers bloom at the Morguefilm Studios.)

### The dangerous game, or where art ends

Once history is written, there is no remaking it. The question is: Can historical truth be found, or is it possible to portray objectively an epoch that no longer exists? Maybe the documents could reveal something. Maybe not. In any event, it should be clear that to unmask a typical British spy or to spank some dead guy's behind is far easier than to examine the dialectics of our own social crises.

In search of successful examples of blending politics and art, I should mention the first films of Eisenstein, the Soviet and German films of the 1930s, and much of Latin American "Third Cinema." But as we look closer, we realize that the "state order" was just a pretext for Eisenstein to work out his own purely aesthetic problems (and he did get away with doing that for a short while). The films of the 1930s, though interesting as a social phenomenon, are, of course, invalid in terms of cinematic art. And, finally, Fernando Solanas and Octavio Getino, the ideologists and creators of the "Third Cinema," never pretended to be artists and openly alienated themselves from any existing cinema.

So one needs to make a firm and conscious choice of whether to be involved in politics or art. Otherwise the corpse in Abel's hands can easily turn into a red banner.

**Keep your tongue between your teeth**

The last part of this article must be devoted to the artistic language of *Repentance*.

There are two clear extremes in film making. The first is *cinema direct*: a camera with a capacious spool is impulsively fixed on a certain angle; a vacant lot where even no bird will fly would be the best. The other extreme is a language of symbols, taken out of context and thus unreadable. Sergei Paradjanov in *The Color of Pomegranates* came close to that edge. Such a method is a step away from signification of ideas, feelings, and characters by figures or even mere evaluation of them by digits as in figure skating.

The cinematic style of *Repentance* is more than accessible. All the symbols are more than simple: the gallows with a raven, the bust of Napoleon, the break in a sewerage system, the medieval knights, the grave in the cage, and so on. Only highlighted sentences and blinking pointers are missing to make it look like educational cinema.

The trouble is that these symbols have no additional meaning to them. They duplicate the context and seem more like labels in a museum exhibit. There is no way to attribute such symbols to artistic imagery.

Yet to be fair I should give a positive example of the director's approach.

There is a scene of the funeral in *Repentance*, which regrettably passes briskly, overshadowing its own brilliance. This scene refers us to the funeral of our former boss, Brezhnev, whose death marked the whole historical period. The television broadcast from Red Square, shot very simply, rang an impressive and dreadful bell to several generations. That broadcast revealed a metaphor, a meaning beyond the event, beyond the phenomenon, beyond the life process.

To recall Bresson, Antonioni, or Wenders would be enough now to realize how shallow and primitive is the simple symbolism used in *Repentance*.

But even this is not the main error of Abuladze. In a picture so precise in recreating Soviet sociopolitical environment of the 1930s and the 1970s, all the symbols slide along the viewer's consciousness as a cheap and useless game. They cause no generalization except the general fear of facts. While the viewer is completely absorbed in recognizing the distinctive marks of reality, the symbols that flash out here and there on the periphery of perception read as obstacles on the way to interpretation.

Not to seem totally negative, I must note that the casting is accurate and, in addition, the two main characters are played by the same actor: not bad! Nonetheless, too much energy has been wasted in unearthing the graves, literally and figuratively.

After all, *Repentance* satisfies the current social order to a considerable extent, for the film is spectacular and politically sharp. Moreover, the movie reflects the condition of that social order, the level of our present social consciousness, the erosion of criteria in this consciousness, which is so confused that it reminds one of the bright colors that, once mixed on an artist's palette, become a gray paste. It is necessary to distinguish those colors by separating the functions of art from those of journalism, political science, and politics. Otherwise, there will be nothing left to do but to hire an excavator and dig up the communal graves.

# Editors' commentary

Tatyana Khloplyankina's coverage of Abuladze's *Repentance*, perestroi-ka's first and perhaps most important feature, must seem to Western readers more a free and easy journalistic piece than anything resembling film criticism. In a fashion typical for Soviet criticism, Khloplyankina builds her argument *around* the film rather than analyzing its text; she conspicuously capitalizes Truth and Spirituality and says nothing about camera or montage. She has a point there: "When a thirsty person sees a spring, this person clings to it without thinking about what this liquid consists of." But however true, this argument does not excuse a critic, even a thirsty one.

Igor Aleinikov, in contrast, belongs to the very generation that, as Khloplyankina writes, cannot live while the mistakes of the past are buried. Ironically, he is not about to "kill himself" over *Repentance*. Neither does he identify with the young hero of the film. While Khloplyankina, who wants *Repentance* to be screened "over and over until everybody believes in democratic ideals," is overtly emotional, almost preachy, Aleinikov, once a leader of the Soviet avant-garde Parallel cinema, is sarcastic, hard hitting, and no-nonsensical in his attack of the film. His piece, published independently in Aleinikov's own underground journal, *Cine Phantom*, turned out to be the only Russian "thumbs-down" review of *Repentance*.

What exists, therefore, between the two views is very much a generational, ideological, and aesthetic conflict. Khloplyankina appreciates *Repentance* as a "big social event," whereas Aleinikov approaches it as a cinematic text to be decoded – an attitude somewhat new for the Soviet critical tradition. More sober and detached from the film's discourse, Aleinikov decisively skips the discussion of Stalinism, its crimes, its victims, or anything in the *subject matter* that would obscure the *film language* of *Repentance*. Instead, he explicitly indicates the root of the film's imperfection. Ironically, it is precisely what, for Khloplyankina, served as a reason not to analyze the film language – the need, as she wrote, to drink before testing the contents of water or, as Aleinikov said, to call a spade a spade.

These reviews are written for different audiences – liberal middle-class

**58**

intelligentsia readers of *Literaturnaya gazeta* (Khloplyankina's employer) and *Moskovskaya pravda* (where her piece first appeared), in the former case, and high-brow, socially disengaged, underground intellectuals in the latter. Both somewhat extremist, these reviews show the range within which the rest of this collection will operate, and so provide a dynamic impulse for our critical marathon.

## CHAPTER II

## Is It Easy To Be Young?

In a sharply polemic manner, the creators of
this feature documentary enter into an open
dialogue with young Latvians. The range of
questions discussed varies from juvenile de-
linquency to the Afghan war. The questions
are dramatized by inability or lack of desire on
the part of the older generation to understand
its children's problems and conflicts.

*Is It Easy To Be Young?* (*Legko li byt' molodym?*). Directed by Juris Podnieks; screenplay
by Abram Kletskin, Yevgeny Margolin, and
Juris Podnieks; cinematography by Kalvis
Zaltsmanis; music by Martinsh Brauns. Color,
83 min. Riga Film Studios production, 1986.

2. The unpopular Afghan War, which left its veterans physically and spiritually crippled, is just one of the previously forbidden youth problems discussed in Juris Podnieks' pioneering feature documentary *Is It Easy To Be Young?* (1986). (Photo: Kinocenter and Sovexportfilm.)

# Is it easy to be grown up?

*Lev Anninsky*

A public discussion was scheduled after the screening. (As far as I know, it was the first preview of *Is It Easy To Be Young?* [1986]) The director, Juris Podnieks, held the show at the Moscow Physicists' Club.

Scarcely had the screening ended and the chairman called for comments when a cry was heard, "May I ask the director a question?" – "Yes, you may." – "Do you consider yourself a naive person?" Juris Podnieks braced himself and answered after a pause with an icy voice, "No, I don't." The questioning continued, "I wonder what you were thinking about? Do you really think this kind of film will ever be released?"

A woman sitting next to Podnieks (she, in fact, was the one who had arranged the session) stood up and began to speak quickly in an agitated tone, as if in a hurry to end this awkwardness, "An Art Council meeting took place today. The film has been approved. The whole film, with no cut-offs."

A heavy silence entered the room. People were digesting the news. I was watching the faces: Come on, dear comrades, say something! While everybody was looking for the right words, I thought of something that made me very uneasy: We have no idea how to react. We are not used to it. If the film had been suppressed, we would not feel lost. We would be outraged. We would demand glasnost. We would shift the blame onto the authorities.

But here it was, out in the open, a film about mad youth, or the "negative phenomena" (as our "great and mighty, truthful and free" Russian language used to label such elements). So come on, speak out! What do you think of it? No, not of the Party control, not of what had seemed like an unattainable glasnost, but of the very substance of the matter.

The audience kept silent, shocked, and confused.

I am convinced that this vacuum of grown-up silence as a response to the wild honesty of the kids on the screen was taken into account by Juris Podnieks in his concept of the film. This documentary has a narrative frame: The interviewees are hard-rock fans who demolished a suburban train after a concert. Armed with iron sticks, they proved to be a crowd of individuals whose discontent we cannot understand. They have no words

63

to explain their own emotions and actions. They talk nonsense. All they seem to want is to destroy or to overturn the world around them, just for the hell of it. However, their attitude touches upon our most painful nerve. We, the grown-ups, have become hypocrites: We think one thing and say the other; we hide behind our masks, but demand sincerity. It is we who have chosen to participate in a play that conflicts with the one the youths are playing.

In relation to this, the film creates a psychological center, a reality that comes to life beyond the screen or, rather, in front of the screen, closer to the audience. This spiritual reality is rooted within the dimensions of the picture, between the lines, at the crossing of the glances cast by those teens who live on the edge.

That reality is exactly where we are at today with all our arrogant contempt for "them," along with their violent values and hidden fears. All we know is how to cunningly use evasive language in which there is but a single label for all they bring along: "negative phenomena." We subconsciously compensate for our lack of self-confidence with violent neglect of "them" who are weaker than we, because they *are* our children. They shave their heads, paint their faces, and wear metal chains on their clothes only to force their way to our hearts, blinded with scorn. Then, of course, they do not know how to say it when we finally agree to listen. But do we ourselves have anything to say? Alas, it would have been easier for us if the omnipresent "authorities" had suppressed the film. We could have complained then that the authorities took away our freedom of speech.

However, the film is released. There is no way out for us. We have to respond out loud to our children who go crazy when they attempt to open a dialogue with us.

# Deafening voids

*Alexander Kiselev*

Take a rubber band and stretch it as far as it goes with one end touching your skin. Let go of the other end. How does it feel? Something similar is happening today with us, as time has suddenly begun to shrink. Time, too, can hurt, and it hurts more than a rubber band.

When trying to characterize contemporary Soviet culture (including film culture), one could not find a better word than *televised*. It is not just that television is the most effective of all the media; it is also capable of conveying the instant miracles of change throughout this ever-changing country. Although Soviet television these days drags behind the newspapers and magazines, other cultural institutions – literature, cinema, rock 'n' roll – bear a distinct sign of this "TV syndrome."

The documentaries that attract the full houses today are most affected by the "TV syndrome." Then again, what is a documentary if not a high-quality news story? Better quality and a bigger budget do not alter the core of the genre. Aesthetics, if not unnecessary, is optional in documentaries.

A good documentary raises the intellectual and emotional temperature to such a degree that the viewer's imagination adds all that is missing in artistic quality. A truly dramatic and sharp documentary may emerge as an event that steps over and beyond its cinematic boundaries. This is what happened to director Juris Podnieks' *Is It Easy to Be Young?*

Since its completion, the film has created a stir comparable to the panic a terrorist act in the heart of Moscow could cause. The film was shown at a plenary meeting of the Latvian Communist Party Central Committee in Riga. Every sequence was discussed, separately and in detail. Podnieks was utterly amazed when the picture was finally approved for national release.

His original idea was to shoot a few interviews with teenagers in which they would share their creeds, dreams, and hopes. After that, Podnieks intended to store the material and resume work on the film ten years later in order to find out what had happened to these kids and their ideals. But during the shoot, the material unexpectedly took over and began to live on its own. The director chose to let his characters shape the project.

The premise was incidental. Returning from another shoot, Podnieks decided to drop by a rock concert featuring a popular Baltic group. At the stadium, the fans, going wild, attracted his attention. He shot a few takes and left. The following day, the news announced that the fans had wrecked the train on the way home, leaving behind a trail of broken windows, torn-up seats, smashed doors. Four out of several hundred involved were put on trial and one was convicted.

The injustice of the hearing, as presented by Podnieks, is even more striking than the grim sight of the ruined train. To pull one person out of the crowd and send him to jail as a scapegoat: Isn't that an act of vandalism on the official level?

In another sequence, a young girl sneaks a dress out of a theater dressing room. She puts it on and goes up to the roof where her boyfriend photographs her. She is caught and charged with theft. During the investigation, she hides her face from the camera and cries, "I was going to return it that same night. I just looked so good in it."

Other sequences present similarly poignant stories:

A chain-smoking young man speaks about his dream of becoming a journalist. Meanwhile, he is working at a morgue transporting corpses. "How do you feel here?" asks Podnieks. "Fine," the young man replies.

A group of punk-rock fans is being expelled from the Academy of Fine Arts for "defiant behavior," that is, for their extravagant clothing and hair styles. They could not fit in anywhere in the buttoned-up society that regards any personal expression as a threat.

Teenagers dressed in long army overcoats and armed with fake rifles are guarding the monument of the Latvian soldiers who defended Lenin and the Soviets during the first communist years. "We're so ashamed!" one of the youths says. "Everybody is staring at us. We feel like total idiots."

Finally, there are the Afghan vets. Survivors of the unpopular war, they live in a vacuum, with no past and a chunk of their future left somewhere in the hills of an alien land. "Why aren't you wearing your medal?" Why bother if no one knows what really happened in Afghanistan, and if it is impossible to answer honestly why there was a war at all?

The film's composition is strikingly traditional and focused on one goal: to let the young people speak. Podnieks uses a gimmick in only the trial sequence – the sound suddenly fades away, then the courtroom audience disappears. We, the film audience, are left alone in dead silence to realize the injustice that has just occurred.

In a visual refrain that runs throughout the film, a man keeps wandering in a labyrinth of corridors. He seems to be looking for someone, but all he finds is his own worthless self. These images do not belong to Podnieks but to an amateur Kafkaesque movie shot by one of his characters. In the coda, the two films coincide: The man finds light at the end of the labyrinth. Along with strange underground creatures standing in water, we see a Baltic Sea sunset. The view stupefies the creatures and fills us with hope and despair. In the end, there are no true answers to the questions raised by the film. Perhaps there are no answers at all.

Sometime in the 1930s, a beautiful temple was blown up in Moscow, the Cathedral of Christ the Savior. The plan was to build a Palace of Soviets in place of it. But Stalin's engineering got so much ahead of itself that it completely forgot how to lay down a foundation correctly. Today, where the Cathedral was, there is the swimming pool "Moscow." So much for atheist ideology.

Obsessed with restoring all that was ruined during the seventy years of the Soviet reign, a group of engineers came up with a proposal to install a holographic image of the cathedral in place of the swimming pool. Although the idea was soon abandoned, the giant hologram could serve as a metaphor and a monument to communist ideology.

When glasnost shattered the thick layers of lies, the Soviet Union's favorite building material, the whole system began to crumble like a house of cards. Society found itself in a vacuum, ready to absorb whatever came its way.

In this deafening vacuum, *Is It Easy to Be Young?* spoke of the void. It was a cry for help and became a blockbuster, leaving behind most of the fiction hits. This was positively the beginning of the "documentary boom" in which history, the economy, crime, politics, and all the rest of our culture was put on trial and reevaluated.

Where do we come from? Who are we and why are we here? What has really happened to us? All these questions had but one answer in the past. Today they need to be addressed as if for the first time, with pluralism and sincerity.

The new documentary has taken this need on as its mission. Style and artistry matter less. The documentary, having become a vanguard of the film culture, is tirelessly injecting truth and reality into the public consciousness. Every month we see a new documentary that could stun the most idle imagination: *The Solovki Regime* (1988), *Confession: The Chronicle of Alienation* (1988), *Is Stalin With Us?* (1988), *The Brick Flag* (1988), *Revolution Square* (1989), and many more.

Glasnost is a process, not a result that can be acquired once and for all. Today we can speak freely about what we could not mention yesterday. And tomorrow we may have the chance to pronounce what might have choked us today.

The artist's courage is what ultimately matters. Much courage is needed for an artist to combat lies, primarily the lies hidden within ourselves. Juris Podnieks is one of those brave artists who manifests how this should be done.

# Editors' commentary

Documentary films have been, without question, the most dynamic, challenging, and memorable of the cinema of glasnost. *Is It Easy to Be Young?* was one of the first and certainly the most popular leader of this new movement.

Lev Anninsky's piece is less a review than a "documentary" of the film's explosion into the Soviet cinemas and, more strikingly, into the Soviet conscience. Anninsky's psychological and spiritual observations are helpful for a Western audience raised on "objective" television documentaries and even the straightforwardly politically biased works such as *Roger and Me* and *Harlan County, USA*.

Whereas Anninsky is an admitted "sixtiesnik" and more a literary, rather than a film, critic, Alexander Kiselev belongs to the younger generation and is a journalist. However, in contrast to the previous duet of critics, these two, despite their differences, complement each other. "Deafening Voids" takes, in Kiselev's hands, a broadly based contextual view of how and where *Is It Easy To Be Young?* fits in. His emphasis on the sense of Soviet and now post-Soviet culture as a "televised" culture places him on the cutting edge of recent critics who are beginning to grapple with the fascinating but complex topic of how the ever-pervasive television set shapes and influences its viewers. Thus, whereas the obvious entry point in discussing the film is the subject matter – troubled youth – Kiselev helps us to see the bigger picture: a fresh attack on bland television documentary by a highly professional and partisan film maker, Juris Podnieks.

Within this context, Kiselev does an excellent job of linking the film to the total collapse of "totalitarian ideology." Here Kiselev hits on the central theme of glasnost documentary and of Podnieks' film in particular: "Podnieks' film speaks of this vacuum created by the awareness of the impossibility of living any further in a universe of lies."

Kiselev's final realization that it is the new and young directors who must come to the front and that, at the moment, it is courage that is more important than art speaks well of his role as a critic judging not only cinema, but also the swiftly shifting glasnost sands in which he wrote his essay.

# CHAPTER III

# A Forgotten Tune for the Flute

A middle-aged Moscow bureaucrat, Filimonov is stagnating in his job and marriage as *perestroika* becomes a reality. While he continues to practice dishonesty in his career, he begins to reawaken as the artist he once promised to be when he has an affair with a nurse. Thrown out of his home by his wife when she discovers his infidelity, he takes up an uneasy residence at the nurse's communal apartment and then, briefly, on the street after she rejects him. When all seems lost, Filimonov's wife takes him back and he gets promoted. But when he sees his former lover on the street, he drops dead of a heart attack, only to be revived by her. Will they live happily ever after?

*A Forgotten Tune for the Flute* (*Zabytaya melodiya dlya fleity*). Directed by Eldar Ryazanov; screenplay by Emil Braginsky and Ryazanov; cinematography by Vadim Alisov; production design by Alexander Borisov; music by Andrei Petrov. Cast: Leonid Filatov, Tatyana Dogileva, Irina Kupchenko, Vsevolod Sanayev, Olga Volkova, Valentin Gaft, and Alexander Shirvindt. Color, 95 min. Mosfilm Studios production, 1987.

3. "Spare some for a former bureaucrat," reads the sign worn by Filimonov (Leonid Filatov), whose career-seeking, self-serving life-style has led him to forget many tunes in Eldar Ryazanov's *A Forgotten Tune for the Flute* (1987), glasnost's first satirical melodrama. (Photo: Kinocenter and Sovexportfilm.)

# Scherzo – suite – nocturne

*Alexander Timofeevsky*

What's our life? A musical piece?
A sonata or a fugue or a mass,
a suite, a nocturne or a scherzo?
                    —Eldar Ryazanov

Director Vladimir Menshov once complained that, until recently, our cinema served tastes of "either the official apparatus or the snobbish elite." When I came across this statement, I almost let myself get upset. Being intimately familiar with Soviet film, I have most certainly missed the instance when it served the "elitist" tastes. When, allow me to ask, did it happen? Which year? Which quarter? Where did this attraction to the "elite" come from? Was it unrequited? Or did the "snobbish elite," paradoxically scornful of its own snobbishness, let itself in turn be ruled by the film industry? And who *is* this "snobbish elite" anyway: black marketeers and hard-currency prostitutes? Please show it to us, so we can see that mysterious audience whose tastes our cinema serves.

Until then, we will stick to our old views. We will keep thinking that such an audience does not exist. Moreover, we will dare to rephrase the earlier statement in a more straightforward way: Until recently, our cinema served no tastes at all. If that is what Menshov wanted to say, then there is nothing to argue about.

Around the world, there is "film auteur" and there is "popular film." Here, the former found itself in trouble, and the latter was hard to find. By definition, film auteur does not serve anybody's tastes; it listens to no one but the Muse. This, however, should not be the rule for popular film. But our cinema "for the masses" was always aimed at some abstract "people," that is, at no one in particular. In this sense, it was unique: film auteur without an auteur, or, strictly speaking, amateur film. In *A Forgotten Tune for the Flute* (1987), writer Emil Braginsky and director Eldar Ryazanov reflected this with a striking metaphor.

The film is pierced by scenes of an amateur female choir sent on tour with an unspecified destination. Two dozen women circle around the country, singing one senseless and meaningless song. They sing it at all latitudes of our immense Motherland: at a picturesque spa with the storming sea as a background; in the storming sea itself; amid the wild, severe mountains. Why, for what sins were they torn away from their workplaces, dressed up in Russian folk costumes, and engaged in choir singing, while they could be first-class tailors and librarians? Neither the "snobbish elite" nor "the official apparatus" is behind it, but some grandiose absurdity, totally self-sufficient and perfect in its own right. What is amazing is not that no one hears their song, but that anyone would bother to come and listen at all. In other words, what is amazing is not that attendance in our movie theaters is decreasing, but that it exists at all. God knows, our people adore their culture.

Unlike the amateur choir of Soviet popular film, Eldar Ryazanov always knows about what, why, and for whom he is making his pictures – a rare directorial quality indeed. This precision is particularly significant for understanding *A Forgotten Tune for the Flute*, with its subtext and hidden drama.

The classic Ryazanov audience – mostly middle-aged, middle-class, and urban – is made up of engineers and researchers, doctors and instructors, that is to say, all those who are usually defined here by the obscure term *technical intelligentsia*. Like everybody else, they were enchanted by *Beware of the Automobile!* (1966), and (unlike the rest of us) they were the ones to whom the director talked during the difficult 1970s in *The Irony of Fate* (1975), *An Office Romance* (1978), and *The Garage* (1980).

The cultural mythology of this audience is quite extensive, although it rests on the three pillars of Bach, the French Impressionists, and Mikhail Bulgakov's *The Master and Margarita*. To be totally honest, we will have to add that this audience calls any organ piece "Bach," that their list of favorite Impressionists begins with Picasso and Modigliani, and that Bulgakov's novel is for them a fount of trivial wisdom. In the 1960s, this audience, poor but proud, jogged properly every day and constantly debated whether figure skating was a sport or an art. Later on, they wished to look healthy and wealthy and, as a reaction to social stagnation, became involved in mysticism. The catalog of things *en vogue* was topped by Syrian furniture à la rococo, yoga, flying saucers, acupuncture, the book *Life After Death*, the film *Memories of the Future*, and endless horoscopes with their benevolent dialectics: "A woman of February is imperious but compliant, a man of March is flirtatious but faithful."

Above all, singing always remained the main value and the most important communal activity of Ryazanov's audience. For them, songs replaced art, religion, money in the bank, often private life, and, until recently, social life. Those were not commercial, loud songs, but quiet, sincere ones, sung among friends in the kitchen or at a campfire.

Eldar Ryazanov's films meant as much for this audience as did songs. Reviewing *A Forgotten Tune for the Flute* (1987), Tatyana Khloplyankina wrote that Ryazanov's films consoled the audience. This is too weak a statement. Those films did not console, they salvaged their audience. They literally gave people back their lost dignity, helped them survive. A notorious, much-written-about hybrid of truth and fairy tale was captured perfectly in Ryazanov's films. They were beautiful enough for one to want to believe in them and true enough for one to actually believe in them.

*A Forgotten Tune for the Flute* – Ryazanov's first film since *perestroika* and about *perestroika* – was meant to redeem the film maker in the eyes of his audience. During stagnation, Ryazanov cheated on his fans in *The Train Station for Two* (1982) and then more explicitly in *The Ruthless Romance* (1984). Ordinary intelligentsia could not accept these films, for the element of identification and recognition of the miracle world, so essential for Ryazanov's relationship with his audience, was missing.

That is why Ryazanov based his next film upon his old play. But along with the tried-out motives, new tones appeared, tones unheard in the director's previous works. Using Ryazanov's own poetic language, one could state that *A Forgotten Tune for the Flute* combines three musical keys: two familiar ones, the satirical (scherzo) and the lyrical (suite); and a new and unexpected one, the mystical (nocturne). And because Ryazanov and cowriter Emil Braginsky conceived the picture as a satire on bureaucracy, "scherzo" was to become its leitmotif.

The action takes place at the fictitious Bureau of Leisure Time, a bureau whose resemblance to our Ministry of Culture is striking. A conflict between the Bureau boss (Vsevolod Sanayev) and his deputy, Filimonov (Leonid Filatov), suggests to the audience that a new-type official may be worse than an old-timer, that the problem of bureaucracy would not be solved by merely replacing one by the other. Unfortunately, this idea, undoubtedly correct, is not developed, and the film sinks into the familiar tones of "an office romance."

Filimonov's milieux – his boss as well as his subordinates, Odinkov (Valentin Gaft), Myasoedov (Alexander Shirvindt), and Surova (Olga Volkova) – are typical characters of a Ryazanov comedy, which could be described by Ryazanov's fans as "a bit funny, a somewhat sad story, told with a mild, kind smile." These character-signs have become so habitual, their reputation so solid that it is difficult to change it. Are they really vicious bureaucrats? Come, come, they are but the warmest hearts.

The absence of real characters and a dramaturgical vacuum turn this film into a revue in which a cue begets only another cue and a joke another joke. These jokes can be funny; certain ones are quoted in almost all the film's reviews (for example, the bureaucrats' anthem, "We don't plough, sow, or make things to order / All we do is take pride in our social order"). Fine, but what about some backbone to support the jokes? The bureaucrats' theatricality could be justified only by a definitive, clearly written leading character. All the rest could have been a vaudeville backdrop. But, alas, the character of the film's lead is nowhere to be found.

Eldar Ryazanov, it seems, could not make up his mind about where such a character would come from – from the satirical, hilarious "scherzo" or from the tender, amorous "suite." Leonid Filatov, the star, is our patented *jeune premier*, and his public image does not coincide with the initial concept of Filimonov as a heartless bureaucrat. In Ryazanov's universe, a leading man, a devoted lover, always deserves a reward. A bad functionary does not. Consequently, Filimonov's romance with the nurse, Lida, makes no headway and remains unresolved. Only Tatyana Dogileva keeps us watching it without ennui.

Lida, the nurse, poor but proud, sharp, and sarcastic, yet sensitive and vulnerable, is played by Tatyana Dogileva with great ease. One should also note, to be fair, that the actress has played this type before, that the type itself has grown old, and, finally, it remains unclear why only nurses and unskilled female workers in our cinema can be bright and sensitive, whereas a general's daughter who is writing her doctoral dissertation cannot.

The part of the general's daughter/doctoral candidate, who is Filimonov's wife (obviously, abandoned), is played by Irina Kupchenko. Here, the peculiar paradox of the picture is most vivid. The role serves to demonstrate that her off-screen father and his important connections would make it impossible for Filimonov to abandon his wife without abandoning the dreams of his boss's chair. This happens in the "scherzo," whereas the morals of the love "suite" make us empathize with the abandoned wife even if she is a general's daughter. According to her function, the wife must play dirty against Filimonov. She has nothing else to do in the "scherzo." But the "suite" amends the play. Her revenge becomes tame, and what comes through is an aging woman with real (if a bit masochistic) pain, wearing an incredible wolf-fur coat. In the end, we cannot decide what causes Filimonov to come back to his wife: pity or his career. If it is pity, it is hard to blame him. Combining a traditional love triangle with an antibureaucratic lampoon, a "suite" with a "scherzo," Ryazanov brings the logistics of one music piece into the other. Naturally, confusion follows. The leading character is the best example.

As the self-absorbed bureaucrat from "scherzo," Filimonov talks about perestroika and bans plays. In the love "suite," he is modest and selfless. Here, he does not reign, but falls victim to circumstances, which places the film's director in a tough dilemma: Filimonov should be punished as a bureaucrat but rewarded as a lover. Ryazanov finds an ingeniously simple solution to this hopeless condition: He kills Filimonov the bureaucrat and revives Filimonov the lover. Enter "nocturne."

Having come back to his wife and taken over his boss's job, Filimonov sees Lida, the nurse, from his office window. Passion inflaming him once again, he drops with a heart attack and is pronounced dead by the paramedics. But Lida, sensing the trouble, rushes into his office, pushes away the doctors, and floods her lover's body with revitalizing tears. Before he opens his eyes, Filimonov goes to purgatory where he meets his late parents and many other interesting species straight out of the book *Life After Death*. The scene is so genuinely pathetic that it leaves almost no hope for director's irony.

Clearly, "scherzo" had to be the leitmotif of a film intended as a satire, and Ryazanov had to realize that overloading the satire with lyricism and mysticism would not bring it closer to the mass audiences. He went for it anyway, rightly assuming that there is nothing wrong with eclecticism, if interpreted artfully. Ryazanov needed eclecticism, and here is why.

The main merit of Ryazanov's films, despite their rigid structures, was always the presence of a certain space that would not submit to rigidity. Critics called it "the air." In the apparent clarity of Ryazanov's films, something was always left unpronounced, untold.

The main value in Ryazanov's films was not what was said, but what was implied or even concealed. *Put In a Word For a Poor Hussar . . .* , a nineteenth-century tale, for example, would hardly benefit from having its action take place in the period of Brezhnev's stagnation, though it was a film about our own troubles and fears. Bunuel once said that all his life he struggled passionately against censorship but only God knows how much he owes it. So does our cinema, whether we like it or not.

The Ryazanov style was molded in *Beware of the Automobile* (1966), his best film, made during the end of Khrushchev's "thaw." The films that followed were more or less euphemistic, but it was precisely in this indirect speech, this play of allusions, pauses, blabbers, and omissions that Ryazanov perfected his artistry. It would be more than naive to think that the freedom of speech that we have been granted recently is a universal cure for all aesthetic problems. On the contrary, new problems are just arising. Any mature artist would have a hard time switching to direct speech, Ryazanov in particular.

In *Forgotten Tune for the Flute*, eclecticism served as an antidote to political obviousness. The "scherzo – suite – nocturne" structure seemed to provide a flexible space with plenty of "air." Besides, the love "suite" was there to support the satirical "scherzo": Ryazanov knows very well that positive identification is quintessential for his relationship with the audience, which had no reason to recognize itself in a vicious high-ranking bureaucrat. But the "scherzo" and the "suite," joined mechanically, interfered rather than supported each other. To save the collapsing structure, Ryazanov resorted to the tactics that had always helped him before: brief and brilliant sketches of urban life. Eager to please the audience, he at times neglected the truth.

Thus, for example, the street artists portrayed by Ryazanov are, in fact, ordinary street hacks and their work is unambitious market fare. In the film, they are avant-gardists and martyrs, pursued by the ignorant bureaucrats who ban daring plays in the daytime and gorge caviar and crabmeat at night. It all seems true and lifelike: Our bureaucrats are ignorant and insatiable indeed, but altogether it becomes nothing but a banal piece of urban folklore, told for midechelon engineers.

*A Forgotten Tune for the Flute* appears to be precisely addressed. A concise encyclopedia of certain tastes and ideas, myths and stereotypes, it seems to have everything Ryazanov's audience requires today. But Ryazanov's old myths worked primarily because they meant more than what was said directly. Now the situation is quite the opposite. All there is to *A Forgotten Tune* can be read about in the newspapers, only there the news is hotter and sharper. The old "air" has evaporated, and the new one has not yet condensed. The "scherzo – suite – nocturne" structure has turned into an arithmetical sum of all the familiar Ryazanov-style elements. But the quantity did not affect the quality. Eldar Ryazanov's direct speech turned out to be – alas! – more vulnerable than his indirect speech.

# Editors' commentary

Though the king of comedy, Eldar Ryazanov is much closer to a Soviet Steven Spielberg – who, as Frank Rich once wrote, has a "genius for giving the public what it wants when it wants it" – than to Woody Allen. For almost forty years, Ryazanov has served as a kind of cinematic radar, responding most sensitively and satisfyingly with his lyrical satires or comic melodramas to the demands of an audience of millions. Alexander Timofeevsky, therefore, could not be more accurate when he chose to examine Ryazanov's work in a cultural rather than a cinematic context.

In this light, Timofeevsky's keen portrait of Ryazanov's own audience (which throughout the last three decades made up a large portion of the Soviet film-going public) is very much to the point. The critic not only pins down this audience as middle-aged and middle-class "technical intelligentsia," which both defines and suggests the limits of Ryazanov's art, but also delineates an "extravert," public-demand-oriented model of film making, which Yuri Bogomolov preaches for in "Cinema for Every Day" and which is so peculiar in the *auteur* culture of "jobless prophets."

Building on his dual analysis – sociological (the audience) and generic (the three genre tiers that form the title of the piece) – Timofeevsky reveals the confusion at the center of Ryazanov's film, which is stuck between the satirical "scherzo," the lyrical "suite," and the mystical "nocturne." Perhaps because of this confusion, *A Forgotten Tune for the Flute* was not only Ryazanov's first perestroika feature but also his last perestroika comedy. His next film, *Dear Elena Sergeyevna* (1988), was a straightforward social drama, as unsophisticated as it was "un-Ryazanov-esque," and his next film, *The Promised Sky* (1991), became the first *post-Soviet* satire.

The critic's verdict of the film's confusion and ultimate failure diagnoses more than the problem of one film: It speaks of the difficulties (even more critical today) of an artist trying to speak in a culture where all the languages suddenly are unleashed.

# CHAPTER IV

# The Cold Summer of '53

Stalin dies in 1953, and a gang of criminals released from a forced labor camp roams into a small northern Russian village. Two political exiles, Chaff (or Luzga) and his older friend, Digger, take on the task of defending the helpless townsfolk. Many, including Digger, die in the final shootout. At film's end, Chaff returns to the city to tell Digger's wife and son of his death, but neither seems particularly interested. As in any classic Western, Chaff walks off alone.

*The Cold Summer of '53* (*Holodnoye leto 53-go*). Directed by Alexander Proshkin; screenplay by Edgar Dubrovsky; cinematography by Boris Brozhovsky; production design by Valery Filippov; music by Vladimir Martynov. Cast: Valery Priemykhov, Anatoly Papanov, Victor Strepanov, Yuri Kuznetsov, Vladimir Kashpur, and Nina Usatova. Color, 101 min. Mosfilm Studios production, 1987.

4. Kopalych (Anatoly Papanov, right) and Luzga (Valery Priemykhov) are political exiles of the late Stalinist period, but when they have to defend their villages from bandits, they play as hard as if they were at the O.K. Corral in Alexander Proshkin's *The Cold Summer of '53* (1987). (Photo: Kinocenter and Sovexportfilm.)

# Birds of passage

*Mikhail Trofimenkov*

"The birds of passage are flying in the blue autumn distance. . . ." This pathetically patriotic Stalinist song could have been played on dozens of turntables in the comfort of a retro fairy tale about totalitarian movie myths. Instead, the song is yelled out to the accompaniment of a boat motor by a bulky fellow wearing an unbuttoned coat, eyes bulging. He has no ear for music, but he does have a submachine gun, and he is overwhelmed by his health and his power over other people's lives. The opening scene, at once alluring and frightening, is a rare gem of true cinema in *The Cold Summer of '53* (1987), one of the most spectacular examples of *glasnost* cinema.

The director Alexander Proshkin is in no rush to inform us who this bulky fellow might be as he steers his film from visual complicity to verbosity and on to a generic confusion of formulas. Who is this man? There are two possibilities, and both make sense, although each answer seems to belong to a different movie.

Let us consider them.

Version one: The bulky fellow is a sheriff, a master of life and death in his territory of law and order. The territory is vast. The northern Russian lands along the coast of the White Sea are spacious and uninhabited. Occasional shootouts still happen there, much in the style of America's Wild West. In the 1950s, when the action takes place, the times were even wilder. Other characters mesh perfectly with the mighty sheriff: an old captain of a perished boat on a canceled route; a cowardly, rowdy supervisor of a trading post; and so on. Naturally there is a sense of danger in the air: six thugs – six outlaws – are hiding in the woods. Of course, they will come to the village, kill the sheriff, rob, and rape. And we suspect that the loneliest and most degraded villager will stand up against the gang. Having mobilized his forgotten power, he will kill all the villains and become the person he had been before the disaster that ruined his life. Such is the Western formula.

We should also note that *The Cold Summer of '53* has much in common with *First Blood* (1982), which was once ostracized by the Soviet critics. Like John Rambo, Luzga, the lead played by Valery Priemykhov, was an intelligence officer during the war, learning how to move unnoticed behind enemy lines, how to kill with a knife or bare hands, how to hide in a tree and jump a foe from the rear, how to survive in the woods on a diet of roots and berries. This guy – an officer, a superman, and a patriot – was badly hurt by his country, lost faith in the people, and wound up embittered and withdrawn. He needed a shock in order to regain human feelings. This is exactly what happens: Through the action and shock, he returns to the embrace of his unfaithful Homeland.

So, is it a Western with a patriotic accent? There is no simple answer. Our film makers have attempted to construct a "Soviet *Rambo*" before glasnost in films such as *Solitary Cruising* (1985). But the story of a virtuous marine fighting somewhere in Polynesia against satanic American imperialists was not only boring, but sickening. How, against the backdrop of such chauvinistic hysterical oeuvres, did this newer retake on *Rambo* not only come closer to the American model in its dramatic structure, but manage to become a classic of perestroika?

Version two: The man on a motorboat is not a sheriff; why use language unfamiliar to a Soviet ear? This guy is a cop, a vet, and a loyal member of the Communist Party. He is bold, and he does not question orders. The soil he is arriving on is not the goldminers' town of the Westerns, but a fishermen's collective farm. Luzga is not hiding here from his disillusionment: He was exiled to this village after serving ten years in a prison camp. He is neither a country bumpkin nor a "green beret," but a victim of political terror. He is one of the millions of Soviet soldiers who were captured by the Nazis, although Luzga's captivity lasted only one day – either because a longer period seemed ideologically unacceptable to the film makers or because such a superman could not bear more than a day in captivity. From there he has moved straight on to one of the islands of the Gulag. The villagers maintain not a human but a class attitude toward him: "No one is put behind bars for nothing." Luzga's companion, another expatriate named Kopalytch, or Digger (Anatoly Papanov), had been a famed engineer before the war. Amazingly, he retained his intellect, curiosity, and habits during his fifteen years in Stalin's camps.

Consequently, in our second scenario, the sheriff, the captain, the salesman, and the poor folks are not just prototypical figures in a genre formula. They are intended to be real people molded in an atmosphere of misery and fear. They cope with life's burdens and hang on to their pants. The bandits are not only the Westerns' dark force clouding the skies but players in the political game that began in 1953 after Stalin's death.

One of Stalin's survivors, Lavrenty Beria, the chief of secret police who was executed later that year, freed hundreds of thousands of criminals from the camps. These "ordinary" criminals (as opposed to the political prisoners) struck towns and villages, leaving a trail of corpses behind. Fighting with them was a tough psychological ordeal, for they, too, seemed to be victims of Stalin. *The Cold Summer* leaves but a clue to this conflict of history and humanity. One of the thugs sings an Ukrainian folk song: Maybe he is a victim of the collectivization that stripped the peasants of their land. Another bandit, a bearded old man, handles a primitive rifle with the familiarity of a peasant who once turned his sickle into a weapon to defend his land from the Bolsheviks. Many details and events in the film bear a trace of social and psychological drama.

The collision of historical honesty and artistic compromise is typical for this period of perestroika. The interest in history is so high that any nod to our horrible past is bound to succeed. It is no laughing matter that for the first time in Soviet film, prisoners have become protagonists. Intellectuals condescendingly comment that despite being superficial and monotonous, the film makers should be praised for introducing the subject of Stalin's camps to the screen. Let people know more about those times, say the prophets of glasnost. The audience will readily put up with a political discourse if a shootout or, even better, a rape scene is coming up. The audience will not go to see a serious social/psychological drama. Director Proshkin knows that, but in search of a balance, he gets lost. The genre he has undertaken is a strong one: The Western is reluctant to give up its rights.

Whereas the social drama works as a vague justification for the shooting, the Western cannot find the energy of its American prototype among the *kolkhozniks* and the victims of Stalin's "personality cult." The film lacks thrills. The confrontations are piled up and ineffective rather than sorted out and choreographed. Furthermore, two key moments – the opening and the final showdown – are blurred. The outlaws arrive in such a hurry that the viewer has no chance to get frightened. We are not prepared for their violent conquest, which makes it hard for us to become involved in the action. In the end, the gang leader who pretended to be dead must face Luzga. But the fight is too brief and confusing to excite. It is as if Proshkin wanted to let us know he is familiar with the rules of the game rather than actually playing by them. At the same time, in trying so hard to make it look real, he forgot to outline the psychology of the drama. For a Western, this psychology is too obvious; for a drama, it is too schematic. Why does a deaf woman play such an important role in the action? Why does her daughter, who a moment ago gleefully chatted with Luzga about going to college, have to die? Why does the head of the trading post team up with the bandits at one point and then try to warn the sheriff at the next?

The film maker's confusion is apparent less in his inability to choose between genres than in his apparent distrust of genres in general. The sheriff tells the captain about the ghostlike appearance of a policeman emerging from the fog on a horse loaded with portraits of Stalin's chief henchman, the displaced and disgraced Beria. This incident could have become a vivid scene in the film, but instead the director chose to present it as a few lines of dialogue. Knowing that the audience will not know the historical details, Proshkin has the sheriff and the captain recount the story of Beria's amnesty for prisoners. And we learn that the gang of outlaws is very dangerous not because of its actions, but from the sheriff's words.

(Of course, in the past, Soviet film makers were not allowed to create Western myths without blatant ideological content. One director, Samvel Gasparov, however, managed to quietly make one Western after the other about the Soviet Civil War, all of them almost completely devoid of ideology. Although he has attracted no serious attention from critics, he has remained professional and honest in his own way.)

As "truth" has become increasingly important for Soviet cinema, film makers feel obliged to reach to the bottom of "realism" on the soundtrack as well as in the image. In *The Cold Summer of '53*, there is a long stretch in which we hear dogs barking. When the barking begins to irritate not only the viewers, but the outlaws, too, they shoot the dogs. In the silence that follows, you can distinctly hear the buzz of mosquitoes and flies. When Luzga, as motionless as an Indian chief, drives away a bothersome fly, we are reminded of the close-up of a fly in the opening of *Once Upon A Time in the West* (1969), the classic example of how a seemingly senseless detail can take on great importance. We soon realize that there are flies everywhere (in both films) and that they help define an atmosphere. At the end of *The Cold Summer* the buzzing of flies is joined by the triumphant screeching of sea gulls and the sounds of a song. This song is repeated three times: at the beginning, during the climax, and at the end. At first we feel we should listen carefully to the lyrics. But after hearing lines about "the birds of passage" three times, we recognize that the director is fascinated more by repetition than by anything else.

Let us now touch upon the film's subconscious subtext. Rambo's revenge was stimulated by his experience in Vietnam. But American cinema demystified the Vietnam War, creating in its smoldering ruins the enchanting baroque fantasies of Francis Ford Coppola. Even Rambo's courage is morbid: He is a victim of the war, a killing machine who longs for love. This could not be said to be the case of our approach to our most important war, World War II. In our collective subconscious, the war is still a forbidden zone. Veterans speak of it as the best time of their lives. There is nothing to be done if life is so dull and sad that the war is the only event worth remembering. Quite a while ago, Jean-Luc Godard protested against the immorality of all war films from *The Longest Day* (1962) to *Ballad of a Soldier* (1959) because they aestheticized war, turning it into a somewhat positive experience. But for the creators of *The Cold Summer of '53*, the war is the only measure by which to test the film's characters. Though the war ended eight years before the story begins, its influence is heavily pushed. The sheriff's voice wavers when he sees Luzga rush for a cigarette butt: "Damn, how can you do that? You've been in the war." And the impassive Luzga stops and pauses a moment: The war unites the guard and the prisoner in one bond. The mention that the sheriff and Luzga fought together against the Nazis makes viewers sympathize with Stalin's troops. In another scene, the old engineer foolishly rises up out of his cover with a weapon in his hands, as if wishing to compensate for the fact that he had no chance to be in the war. It is then all right for him to die, and he does.

And, finally, just as Rambo subconsciously superimposes memories of his Vietcong tortures over the torments he receives at home, so Luzga has memories that cast a Nazi shadow over the Russian outlaws. Did one of them really shout "Hande Hoch!" or was it the grim memory of a former intelligence officer come back to haunt him? Another image even more clearly manipulates Soviet viewers raised on ideological cliches. The fugitives brandishing submachine guns force the villagers into huts and lock them up. This scene, complete with puffs of smoke and melancholy music, is a flash quotation from our partisan film genre in which German soldiers often burn peaceful villagers locked inside their homes. Alas, despite its innovation in previously banned subject matter, *The Cold Summer of '53* remains within the circle of stereotypes.

The dwelling upon Soviet cliches comes to a climax in the film's epilogue. The exonerated Luzga returns to the city to visit Kopalytch's family. Afterward, as he wanders in a park, he recognizes in an occasional passerby a kindred exonerated soul. Cinematically effective, the scene provides Luzga and us with only one visual clue: The stranger carries exactly the same suitcase Luzga does; he is also a traveling soul, an outcast with no roof and no roots. Unfortunately, this image is accompanied by the same obtrusive song about the birds of passage. The birds "are flying to distant countries, but I am staying with you, my Native Land. I don't want the coast of Turkey, and I don't want Africa either. . . . I will go through it again." Apparently, our native prison camps are better than the Turkish coast, and the Motherland gets forgiveness for all its crimes in advance. Rambo at least was more honest. He shouted, "I want America to love me as much as I love her." This Soviet Rambo is not as articulate. The idea that the Afghanistan experience, for example, might be "overcome" by the Soviet cinema in such a simplistically "patriotic" way remains horrifying.

Stylistic consistency is nowhere to be found in *The Cold Summer.* The conformist film language, employing visual and ideological stereotypes, is hopelessly dead. A renaissance of our cinema will come not through the illustration of newly revealed facts, but through radical experiments with language, cinematic and verbal.

As for our tragic past, it is absurd and grotesque. Sacrifice and evil, sadism and buffoonery are so mixed up, and the scope of events so improbable that the most adequate form of its representation just might be a spaghetti Western, full of shocking visual images and totally devoid of any simplistic moralizing.

# Editors' commentary

Time will surely hold up the judgment that *The Cold Summer of '53* was a unique cinematic experiment of the early *glasnost* period. Not only did director Alexander Proshkin try to find a way to deal with the Stalinist past in a gripping narrative, but he also attempted to make a "Russian" film and a *perestroika* film while borrowing from the Hollywood genre formula. However, having stopped halfway, Proshkin produced a film centaur with the head of a Western and the body of a historical drama.

Mikhail Trofimenkov captures this duality well in both what and how he writes about the film. The youngest of the contributors to this collection, Trofimenkov stands out among Russian critics as being one of the few who takes a direct, intense look at the film itself. His close analysis of the first scene opens up the rest of the work for him and for us in two possible interpretations of one image.

This is not a folksy piece in the style of the old school, full of personal anecdotes and stories, moralistic sequences and spiritual invocations. Rather, Trofimenkov is a serious student of cinema, concerned with how culture and genre work and do not work together. A card-carrying "postmodernist" and a respected voice in the "new criticism," Trofimenkov, who writes about cultural mutants and AIDS as well as about painting, music, and film, chooses cultural rather than social, historical, or existential coordinates, genre rather than life, and Rambo rather than the terrors of Stalinism as his critical orientation. A writer with a finely tuned ear as well as a keen eye, Trofimenkov produces a fair critique, perhaps the most even-handed in our collection in capturing the virtues and foibles of both one transitional film and the whole transitional period.

A young rock singer, Bananan, falls in love
with Alika, a teenage siren and a mistress of a
Soviet Mafia godfather figure. Elements of
drama, American gangster films, and cheap romance lead to a thrillerlike chase and a final
bloodbath in which both men die. Also interwoven through this collage are dramatic re-
creations of the murder of Tsar Paul I.
Throughout the film, songs by once-banned
rock groups, especially Aquarium and Kino,
fill the soundtrack.

*Assa*. Directed by Sergei Solovyev; screenplay
by Sergei Livnev and Sergei Solovyev; cinematography by Pavel Lebeshev; production
design by Marxen Gauhman-Sverdlov; music
by Boris Grebenshchikov. Cast: Sergei (Africa)
Bugayev, Tatyana Drubich, Stanislav Govorukhin, Alexander Bashirov, and Victor Tsoi.
Color, 152 min. Mosfilm Studios production,
1987.

5. Sex, rackets, and rock 'n' roll are the ingredients of *Assa* (1987), Sergei Solovyev's postpunk glasnost gumbo, featuring director Stanislav Govorukhin as a cool godfather figure and Tatyana Drubich as his young, unearthly moll. (Photo: Kinocenter and Sovexportfilm.)

# The tenderest shroud

*Alexander Timofeevsky*

In a radio interview, director Sergei Solovyev called his film *Assa* (1987) "a cheap area rug with strands of Bach woven in." To translate this poetic expression into the boring language of film criticism would be to say that in *Assa*, Solovyev has turned positively to the aesthetics of postmodernism. Deliberately eclectic, the film combines disjointed elements – a detective story, a melodrama, and other "lower" genres – and employs all with a high goal in mind. It flirts with kitsch and pop culture, alludes to real and made-up quotations (often knowingly meaningless), and mocks everything, including the most popular notions.

The term "postmodern" is still quite unpopular here. So are such synonyms as "the new eclecticism," and "pluralistic style." Instead critics call it "a multilayered Napoleon pastry."

Five layers are easily discernable in *Assa*. The first is the detective story, which involves a crook named Krymov, the cops, the mob, and KGB agents. The second is melodrama; it centers around the triangle of an aging mobster, his young lover, and a rock 'n' roll kid, Bananan. Layer number three, that of rock 'n' roll culture, includes songs by Boris Grebenshchikov, the underground design of Bananan's chamber, his avant-garde-style dreams, and so on. The fourth layer, seemingly unexpected, contains a reenactment of the assassination of Tsar Paul I, a parody on history shot in a vigorously theatrical style. Finally, there is the top or bottom layer (depending on one's point of view), the finest and most significant one. It is created of the whimsical combination of all of the preceding: not a historical anecdote, but our recent hilarious history, a tragifarcical image of Brezhnev's "stagnation" as seen in the southern city of Yalta, buried under the snow in the winter of 1980.

*Assa* had just opened theatrically when the critics rushed to judge it by standards totally irrelevant to it. The only question asked was: Is it true to life or not? In an *Izvestiya* (February 8, 1988) article, "Is It Easy to Be? . . . " Stanislav Rassadin wrote,

*Assa* depicts a world in which a young woman, being a lover of a monstrous criminal and murderer, can remain touchingly, vulnerably pure. . . . I am either supposed to believe that one can peacefully and even amorously coexist with an ostentatious incarnation of Evil and Crime without losing one's soul, or, as I prefer from a moral standpoint, the film makers do not count on my (and the heroine's) ability to identify this familiarly Americanized type of gangster with all his irresistible negative charm and showy wealth.

Equipped with his critical ability and experience, Rassadin could have identified more than just the familiar Americanized gangster. The movie makes it clear that the gangster, his mistress with her alien looks and unearthly name, Alika, and the rock 'n' roll kid – a young chevalier, a poor but proud romantic admirer – are all character signs, modified masks from a cheap romance novel who, by definition, cannot be expected to act with psychological authenticity. Curiously, the hip style does not camouflage but reveals the signified. Does not Bananan's earring with Alika's picture in it serve as a fair lady's handkerchief from a classical romance?

The movie also makes it clear that this triangle is doomed to a bloody finale, predetermined by the logistics of the criminal melodrama. The film makers do not intend to hide this from us; on the contrary, a rifle that Alika unloads into her lover's head in Act Five has appeared, as it should, in Act One. Of course, the bleeding Krymov collapses on the roses (scarlet blood on scarlet flowers), spread meticulously underneath him, by no accident. Developing the melodramatic line, Solovyev consistently mocks and plays with the canons of a cheap romance, both aesthetic and ethic. According to the latter, a gangster's mistress must keep her soul and purity intact. After all, what else could she do? Should she start drinking forgetfully or report on her lover to the KGB? Then it would have been a morality tale, not a romance.

It seems Rassadin may have suspected that his claims on psychological authenticity were not relevant. Note the use of the word *playroom* in the following excerpt from his review: "According to the skillful director's concept, life in *Assa* is not life at all but a playroom. What do we find there? There is a dwarf theater, a theater of all theaters, . . . a shooting gallery that resembles a theater; and interiors that don't resemble those we live in." We could also add here a boat, a hotel, a racetrack, and a restaurant, which also caused reproaches from the champions of "life as it is." But there must have been a reason for the hardboiled detective, the cheap melodrama, the dwarfs, and all the locales, topped by the snowy Southern town, to appear equally important to the director. To realize that, we must first find out what *Assa* is all about.

In the film *A Mirror for a Hero* (1988), two contemporary characters find themselves in 1949, living through one day that keeps recurring. By this narrative technique, Stalinist Russia is presented in an Orwellian light as a realm of everlasting absurdity and never-ending hell. The route, chosen by screenwriter Nadezhda Kozhushanaya and director Vladimir Khotinenko, is not entirely aimless, although the departing point – the metaphor itself – is arguable. The repeating day symbolizes global stagnation that did not, in fact, exist in Stalin's time; the seven-year period between the end of the war and Stalin's death in 1953 was full of changes and events. Life was far from boring: Every day brought a new decree, a new trial, or a new enemy. Whereas the senile Brezhnev's time was a metaphor for dull stagnation, Stalin's time was a romantic and murderous adolescence. That is why the sculpture by Vera Mukhina, "Worker and Peasant," has become its symbol. A fine contamination of two classical pieces, "Harmodius and Aristogethos" and "Nike of Samothrace," Mukhina's sculpture mesmerizes, aside from the aesthetic qualities, by its pagan purposefulness, and furious blast toward the nightmarish "bright future."

Whereas any normal society develops within the context of the past, present, and future, the Stalinist era knew only the future, and the Brezhnev period only the present. *Assa*, the first historical drama about the stagnation years, depicts that Brezhnev Present – a middle with no beginning or end, an overwhelming, crazy, still-born Present, as horrifying and dull as it was phantasmagorical and poetic.

During that twenty-year-long day, all words lost their meaning, all faces their color. Man had become a werewolf whose appearance, soul, and purpose proved incompatible with one another, a series of ever-changing masks in a hazy world of the total Present. Cliched signs of cheap romance – an "aging lover," a "tender paramour," a "romantic admirer" – are the only substances one could grasp in this unreal world where the characters–phantoms, people–mirages make their endless rounds. Common sense could not help us comprehend and explain this world. Even if we took for granted that the wiseguy is a graduate of the Foreign Languages Institute and a published poet, even if we accepted that he reads historical novels and quotes Pushkin between his crimes, it would be hard for us to believe that he is known in the mob as Swann, a lover from Proust (a questionable source for nicknames). All the same, this *is* reality, not a shallow lifelike reproduction, but the absurd, still-born reality of the time.

Consider: A nurse from the remote town of Oryol has the mannerisms of a big-time movie star; the "star" of the local hotel wears a police uniform; an Air Force captain turns out to be a thug; a thug turns out to be a KGB agent; and a Russian negro spends winter in southern Yalta where the tropical palm trees spend winter buried under the snow – *Assa* makes this unnatural world look not only natural but harmonious. The camera of virtuoso cinematographer Pavel Lebeshev nourishes the unity and self-sufficiency of this world as much as it captures its perverse beauty.

To his credit, Solovyev resists the temptation to use Soviet "soc-art" to portray the period of stagnation. "Soc-art," a style in nonconformist painting, previously illegal, parodies Soviet sociopolitical mythology, with all its parades, slogans, speeches, and informers. Over the past few years, "soc-art" has been spreading to music, literature, and film. Had Solovyev used it, we would have seen a fake blonde with a triple chin and gold teeth standing under the poster "Communism is Inevitable" and singing a 1970s hit about "hope as our reward for courage." The image could have been a bit funny and a bit sad, but it could not have possibly been as colorful and ridiculous as its prototype.

By employing very few elements of "soc-art," Solovyev avoids turning *Assa* into a political joke. He multiplies playful tricks and brings the dwarf actors into the limelight. These heavily made-up toy creatures who sing old Vienna operetta on the frozen summer stage for the two-and-a-half-viewer audience, embrace the image of a fake blonde with her "hopeful" song, but signify something more than that.

The dwarfs with their doll-like happiness are the symbol of yearning in this snowy tropics where one day lasts forever. Cheap cots in wretched theatrical hostels, luxurious suites in expensive hotels. The shooting gallery. The restaurant. The racetrack. The botanical garden. Shabby imperial grandeur. A storm. On the shore, nausea is the same as on the deck, whether it is caused by anguish, boredom, or hatred:

And the sailor, cast not in the crew,
Staggers through the storm.
All is lost, all's drunk to the bottom!
Enough, I can't take it any more. . . .
And the beach of a deserted harbor
Is buried under the first light snow. . . .
In the clearest, in the tenderest shroud
Do you, sailor, have sweet dreams?
                                    —Alexander Block

In the kitschy aesthetics of postmodernism, set largely in a "playroom" where any statement threatens to turn into its antonym, anything goes – anything, that is, except romanticism that lacks irony and psychology that is too deep. *Assa* suffers from both.

The critics who rejected *Assa* for the gaps in psychological truth unanimously praised the scenes at the police station and in the jail – to my mind the best argument for the excessiveness of those scenes. Rassadin writes:

There is, of course, truth in the film, a bitter, tough and even cruel truth. Consider the sequence at the police station where the protagonist is being punished for an "unmanly" earring. Or, take the faces in the audience as they stare with greedy curiosity at the dwarves' show, which profits from human anomaly. The heart aches at such moments, painfully but gratefully. But strangely enough, these moments of empathy, just given to us, are immediately taken away.

The audience's faces are quite expressive and quite necessary. They throw us back into reality by switching the rules of the game, by incorporating the images alien to the playroom tricks. The brief and beautiful scene in which a widowed dwarf woman is visited by her nondwarf son delivers the same shock to us. However, the very strength of these sequences is in their being "immediately taken away." The same cannot be said of either the jail or the police station sequences. Detailed, thorough, and very convincing psychologically, those sequences are quite lifelike, and that is exactly why they are hardly necessary. They would do well in any psychological drama, but in the lightweight, ephemeral, playful, whimsical, and phantasmagorical *Assa*, they seem out of place.

Stanislav Govorukhin, who plays the wise guy Krymov so expressively he seems to be aiming at a Best Actor award, is less convincing in the playroom of *Assa* than Tatyana Drubich as Alika and Sergei Bugayev as Bananan, whose acting according to any conventional standards is poor. We are faced with the choice: psychologically rich acting or *Assa* itself.

The second foible of *Assa* is perhaps even more essential. Sergei Solovyev has gone a long way from the solid moral axioms of his previous film, *The Heiress* (1982). He has arrived at his remarkable playroom, but he has done so by means of rock music, that is, something alien to his sensibility. Rock 'n' roll proved to be a fruitful but fatal injection for *Assa*.

Passionately, Solovyev fell for rock 'n' roll and got trapped by it. At times, it feels like the material rules the director and not the other way around, which is always a problem, especially in the aesthetics of kitsch. As a result, the accents have shifted, and the closing shot of the crowd gathering to see rock star Victor Tsoi became one-dimensional, despite its significance. The whole discourse turned into an apologia for rock 'n' roll, overwhelming the historical theme and botching the "Napoleon"-like equity of the layers.

Not to sweeten the pill, but for the sake of truth, I should note in conclusion that time is working for *Assa*. The hoopla around the film will quiet down along with the rock 'n' roll boom. The film will find its cultural niche where only the beautiful images created by Solovyev will remain: storm and dead calm, palm trees under snow, and a hazy town under the "tenderest shroud."

# Editors' commentary

David Bordwell has complained in *Making Meaning* (Cambridge, Mass.: Harvard University Press, 1989) that there is not enough confrontational dialogue in American film criticism and theory. Such could not be said to be true in the film criticism of the *glasnost* and post-*glasnost* periods, as demonstrated by Alexander Timofeevsky's polemical essays and reviews, three of which are reprinted in our collection. In "The Last Romantics," he strikes at the utopian mentality of Khrushchev's "thaw" ideologists; in his review of *A Forgotten Tune for the Flute* (1987), he launches a feisty attack on popular director Vladimir Menshov for his claim that a "snobbish elite" rules Soviet cinema; in his review of *Assa*, his target is Stanislav Rassadin and other critics who would be ready to disgracefully discharge any movie that does not have a psychologically justified and lifelike subject matter. Aside from wit and sharpness, the only common denominator for the Timofeevsky offensives is that they all are aimed at the "sixties-niks," who, in spite of Timofeevsky's own adieu to them in "The Last Romantics," remained the leading social and cultural force of *perestroika*. In the late 1980s and early 1990s, Alexander Timofeevsky was one of the few young critics who stood up for their generation, confronting the elders with new aesthetic credo and new critical apparatus.

*Assa* was, when it appeared in 1987, the perfect test case for critics and audiences to react to, with for, or against. Sergei Solovyev, the director as well as one of the first independent Soviet producers, helped fuel the dialogue by presenting his film as a "happening" complete with pop art exhibits, parties, rock concerts. *Assa* helped the young generation begin to find a language of its own with which to speak of postmodern art and culture.

At the same time, *Assa* – quite an imperfect work of film art – presented the critic with a complicated case: The apparent intentions of the film maker were exciting, healthy, and promising for the future of Soviet film, while the result was rather weak. (Marina Drozdova, reviewing *The Needle* in the piece presented in Chapter IX, found herself in a similar situation.) What should an honest critic do in such a case: ruin a needful trend or praise a frail work of art? Timofeevsky, the strongest supporter of Solovyev's innovations, resolved this tricky dilemma with the high degree of professionalism. He critiqued the director for the confusion in both the narrative and the genre levels of *Assa*'s "Napoleon-pastry" structure, as well as for his lack of true understanding of rock culture. Nevertheless, he rightly placed *Assa* in the context of glasnost as one of the most important beginnings of the new cinema.

# CHAPTER VI

# Commissar

During the Civil War in the 1920s, Red Army troops enter a small Southern town that they have just retaken from the Tsarist White Guard. Unexpectedly, it turns out that the squad commissar, Klavdia Vavilova, is pregnant. The commander decides to put her up in a slum hovel belonging to a tinker, Yefim Magazanik. It is rather hard for the commissar to get on in the strange milieu of a large Jewish family. Besides, her upcoming motherhood appears to her as an unfortunate encumbrance to military service. But time passes, the commissar becomes a mother, and this unsmiling, stern warrior grows soft and womanly. But soon the White Guard has taken the offensive and the Reds have to leave town. Vavilova faces a dilemma: stay and wait for better times, or leave the child with the family who sheltered her and return to the ranks. She chooses the latter.

*Commissar (Komissar)*. Directed by Alexander Askoldov; screenplay by Askoldov (based on the short story "In the Town of Berdichev" by Vasily Grossman); cinematography by Valery Ginzburg; production design by Sergei Serebrennikov; music by Alfred Schnittke. Cast: Nonna Mordyukova, Rolan Bykov, Vasily Shukshin, and Raisa Nedashkovskaya. Black and white, 109 min. Gorky Studios (1967)/ Mosfilm Studios (1987) production.

6. In Jewish tinker Yefim Magazanik's (Rolan Bykov, center) nightmarish flash-
forward, the Jews of the early 1920s are led to the gas chambers of the 1940s in
*Commissar* (made in 1967, released in 1987), Alexander Askoldov's visionary
tale of love, war, maternity, and betrayal. (Photo: Kinocenter and Sovexportfilm.)

# Commissar

*Maya Turovskaya*

The credits are studded with stars and celebrities; the cast includes such famous actors as Nonna Mordyukova, Rolan Bykov, and Vasily Shukshin. The composer is Alfred Schnittke and the screenplay is based on a story by Vasily Grossman titled "In the Town of Berdichev."

The film extends the boundaries of the story, which is limited in space and time. Although carefully preserved, the main strands in the narrative have been greatly enlarged by Alexander Askoldov, who wrote the script and directed the film.

The town of Berdichev looks big on the screen. It has a Russian Orthodox church, a Catholic church, and a synagogue. No wonder the people who gather in the marketplace are a motley crowd. In the opening sequence, the city is desolate and deserted, as is always the case when the government changes, and here it has already changed fourteen times. When Commissar Klavdia Vavilova enters the city at the head of her battalion, the first thing she does is to shoot a deserter who had escaped home to his wife. The milk from a jug he had been clutching to his chest mixes with his blood.

The scene is not to be found in the original story, but the director has extracted it from the atmosphere surrounding Grossman's text. The same is true of the cosmopolitan, multilingual population that preaches different religions and is accustomed to a succession of governments and invasions. The contrasts between peace and war, ordinary life and revolution, the eternal and the transitory, life and death, milk and blood are highlighted by the anecdote about the straight-laced commissar Vavilova, who has to take a leave of absence to give birth to her baby in the house occupied by the Jewish tinker Yefim Magazanik and his large family. In the end, she follows her retreating battalion and leaves her baby with the kindly, reliable Maria.

Vavilova is played by Nonna Mordyukova, Magazanik by Rolan Bykov, and Maria by Raisa Nedashkovskaya, who is able to hold her own opposite that brilliant duo.

The story is told by Grossman without sentimentality, in a stark and terse form. Making an adaptation, a film maker could emphasize the raw,

**99**

lusty colors of everyday life, or he could choose the romantic revolutionary spirit. He has chosen both.

I think that Askoldov's film – for all the unmistakable signs that it was made in the 1960s – has not aged a bit, precisely because, like the author of the original story, the director keeps a perfect balance. As a person involved in historical events, Commissar Vavilova behaves according to the logic of the revolution: duty, violence, and self-sacrifice. As ordinary people, the tinker Magazanik and his noisy family are preoccupied with their daily troubles, with births, with deaths, and with love. The film juxtaposes the domes and spires of various cathedrals, and the Russian and Jewish lullabies, just as it does the squalid but warm and homey air of the place with the severe, ascetic, masculine life of the combatants. That life is also picturesque in its own way, here it is embodied in the heavy figure of the leather-jacketed regiment commander, played by Vasily Shukshin.

The juxtaposition is dramatic and harrowing for it reflects a social cataclysm. Vavilova was born to be a woman – the actress shows how motherhood makes her beautiful – but she cannot fully enjoy motherhood. Magazanik was born to love his wife and life. The actor shows his extraordinary capacity for love in a short scene of a peaceful morning. But it is unlikely that he will live to see a streetcar running in his native Berdichev. War upsets the peaceful rhythm of life: The horrors of a town constantly changing hands are shown through the games the Magazanik children play. Vavilova has to abandon her baby son, to get into her jackboots, take up her gun, and catch up with the battalion retreating along a deserted street.

It is hard to be human in a world turned upside down. But the director and the cast manage to find various degrees of humanity in their characters without idealizing them. That is why the story of a female warrior who becomes pregnant has a tragic tone to it.

While you rejoice that the film, back on the screen after being shelved for twenty years, has lost none of its freshness, spare a thought for the film maker, who had been banned from making films for twenty years. Tragedies, even if they have a happy ending, happen not only on the screen.

# Editors' commentary

Perhaps no other Russian critic has demonstrated such a multifaceted talent over so long a period as has Maya Turovskaya, the Susan Sontag of Soviet aesthetic thought. There is a sense of almost effortless prose in her writing, whether she is writing a book-length study of Tarkovsky or James Bond and other pop-culture myths, or simply a short review. There is a comforting clarity, straightforwardness, and lack of mystification in her criticism. It is confident and informed, but never lecturing. Because Turovskaya, a drama critic first, understands theater so well, she is better than most critics at appreciating film as performance. A connoisseur of belles lettres as well, she is always attentive to the literary core of a film. Lastly, a culture critic at large, Turovskaya knows exactly how to place a piece of art into its cultural context.

That said, she cuts to the essence of *Commissar* and this long-shelved film's nonpolitical ideology: "It is hard to be human in a world turned upside down." She also precisely identifies the complete lack of sentimentality and yet the strong emotions that the film evokes.

Clearly, in such an analysis, content is emphasized and the aesthetics of Askoldov's remarkable cinematography are downplayed. Much could be made of his uncluttered mise-en-scène, his haunting use of montage, and his uncompromising black-and-white images. But if Turovskaya, one of the brightest and most sincere voices of the post-Stalinist generation, had to make a sacrifice to a tight format (as is the case here), it would always be formal finesse, and not the truth she gave away.

# CHAPTER VII

# Little Vera

Vera is a young woman in the small industrial wasteland of a Ukrainian city who lives with her working-class family in a crowded apartment and dreams of a better life. Though a local "good" boy likes her, she rejects him in favor of a young student, Sergei, who becomes her lover and then fiancé. When efforts to introduce him to her family prove to be a disaster, Vera attempts an overdose of booze and pills only to be rescued by her successful Moscow-based brother and Sergei. At film's end, Sergei is moving in with her and her father keels over of a heart attack.

*Little Vera* (*Malen'kaya Vera*). Directed by Vasily Pichul; written by Maria Khmelik; cinematography by Yefim Reznikov; production design by Vladimir Pasternak; music by Vladimir Matetsky. Cast: Natalia Negoda, Andrei Sokolov, Liudmila Zaitseva, and Yuri Nazarov. Color, 135 min. Gorky Studios production, 1988.

7. Vasily Pichul, director of the glasnost smash hit *Little Vera* (1988), never forgets that Vera also means "faith" as he observes the drama of his heroine (Natalya Negoda, left). (Photo: Kinocenter and Sovexportfilm.)

# Forward, singing!

*Tatyana Moskvina*

There are planes that take off without needing a runway. So it was when director Vasily Pichul and scriptwriter Maria Khmelik launched *Little Vera* (1988). Somehow they escaped all meetings and conferences, all special places where young cinema is supposed to be "bred." They bypassed all the rules and made no promises; they just created a clever, bold film. They made it as if there were no cinema before them, as if they saw everything for the first time.

There was a lot of talk among critics about *Little Vera* being a true slice of life, about the conflict of parents and children. This truth is too obvious not to be boring. As a matter of fact, all the fascination of the film – its unique charm – is in another direction.

The barbarous, savage freshness of *Little Vera* is the originality of a talent that creates not a schematic diagram (however clever and convincing), but the rich, full picture of life.

The film begins with a panorama of a town: newly erected buildings under tirelessly smoking chimneys. Here is a beach by a sea, within city limits, cluttered with rusty constructions and concrete slabs. It is the southern town of Zhdanov/Marioupol, once a bountiful land. But whatever you call this town – Zhdanov was the main ideologist of Stalinist era, Marioupol a tender ghost of the prerevolutionary – you can find its twin everywhere. This is our standard Soviet town, and the film makers do not dress it up to look more attractive.

Experts claim that everyday southern life is presented by director Pichul with the precision of a passionate ethnographer. Meanwhile, all the substantial details are condensed in *Little Vera* into one image, the image of being.

What usually occurs in art displaying banal, tense, and mechanical, that is, ordinary existence, is a cheerless and convicting tone. There is nothing of that in Pichul's picture.

This life is as strong as a rock and as juicy as a ripe watermelon. Homemade vodka is kept here in gallon jars, the smallest volume available, and measured with a scoop from a pan. A slim girl beats up a policeman as no fellow can do. Dancing turns to fighting. The town's inhabitants drink,

**105**

fight, and cry; they love each other, and it is not a Platonic love at all. Although the short erotic sequence in the film has stirred up many Soviet viewers, it is not only appropriate, but required: This world is overflowing with sensuality, emotions, passions. In the house of Vera's friend (I hope there will be a chance to see such an eccentric and gifted actress as Alexandra Tabakova again), her black brother wanders around – a consequence of fierce interracial passions of the past. And Vera (Natalia Negoda), a beautiful savage with a radiant smile and plastic jewelry, is the personification of young sensuality.

Idiotic, yes, but a lively and passionate world. They cannot speak normally; they yell when they dislike something, or hit one another in the face, or throw an ashtray, or stab with a knife. "It is a cruel and wild world, but it has nothing to do with decay, degradation, degeneration," wrote one Russian critic of the last century about a text portraying the people's life. Since that time, Russian life had changed radically. It has lost everything: religion and ritual, soul and crafts but, as *Little Vera* indicates, not its tremendous energy. Purposeless, perhaps, but wildly passionate nonetheless. Here is no place for reasonable activity or spiritual efforts – it is an absolutely brutal life though not a hopeless one: the charm of youth, the desire of love, even sudden grief make it promising.

If *Little Vera* had appeared earlier, it would have been accused of slandering the ordinary Soviet citizen. The casting of Liudmila Zaitseva and Yuri Nazarov as Vera's parents is far from random. Zaitseva used to be a patent "simple, heartfelt woman" of the Soviet screen; Nazarov was a well-known "brawny, reliable guy." *Little Vera* turned their stereotypes upside down: They play their roles so dashingly, so sharply, so bitterly that the viewer is left dumbfounded. It is hard to forget the father growing flabby in drunken complacency or becoming bestially violent: He is at once disgusting and pitiful. And long after the film ends, you remember the mother with her vacant, almost automatic thriftiness and the panicky terror on her face when someone refuses to eat.

Brave little Vera, of whose barbarious beauty I was completely convinced by Natalia Negoda, is of this life, an offspring of her parents. She suffers subconsciously from her family ties, but even her dreamily handsome lover (Andrei Sokolov), almost improbable in his prettiness, cannot draw her away from her roots. She just as easily vents her anger on others, and her sensual aggressiveness gets along perfectly with her inherited narrow-mindedness.

That is why little Vera bursts out sobbing under a cloudburst of biblical proportions, embracing her father after he nearly kills her lover. It is the end of love and life, which she forgives and accepts.

The director, however, loves his characters so tenderly that the most dreadful things, seemingly fatal, finally recede. Sergei is alive, Vera is alive, and even the father's lonely death from a heart attack gives him the tragic right to sympathy.

So was it worth Vera's having been impudent, teasing, and insulting? The older generation needs so little to be content: to talk frankly, to drink decently, to eat their fill. But Soviet kids attach excessive importance to their folks: whether worshiping or rejecting them. And the extremism of youth is the other side of their parents' barbarity. As one of the characters in Chekhov's notebooks says, "Why don't you, mother, stay away from my guests: you are too fat." Vera's parents are unable to understand, but neither are her brother and her fabulous and contemptuous lover. Clearly, any appeal to love each other would be comic and irrelevant here, but the film fortunately avoids a didactic tone. What it depicts instead is a breaking of ancient ties, family ties; even if this break is justified, the fruits of it can only be tragic.

Yet *Little Vera* is not a tragedy. Its genre, seemingly shapeless, is multifaceted. It combines satire and comedy with melodrama and even "criminal tango." This cocktail, however, is far from mere eclecticism. With its pagan freshness and direct relation directly to our life and our art, it presents the new stage in Soviet cinema.

This stage could be called "cinema-zero" because it has to start off from the very ground. This new film is tightly and vitally linked with the surface of current reality, and it does not mystify reality, portraying it "as it should be." On the contrary, its critical zeal focuses on the humorous aspects of life and finds them everywhere.

Besides, *Little Vera* is a step toward the liberation of Soviet film actors. The director did not set them any false tasks, so they could combine the truth of satire with the truth of real feelings and emotions. Their performances lack any gaps: In *Little Vera*, we see a rare richness of acting.

The commercial success of *Little Vera* was spectacular. Khmelik and Pichul's mocking, sharp, dramatic, and unpredictable film shows a talent that stops at nothing and breaks through everything. So "forward, singing," as Vera's father says before he swallows a glass of vodka and as Vera whispers, facing the combat of love and death.

# Editors' commentary

Tatyana Moskvina's celebration of *Little Vera* (1988) will most likely receive more attention from readers than most reviews in this collection, if for no other reason than that *Little Vera* has reached a wider audience in the West than any other *glasnost*-period Soviet film. Readers will thus be able to judge for themselves how completely Moskvina's review fits in with the Russian critical tradition of "intuitive" criticism outlined in the introduction.

There is no discussion of feminism and women's rights (the topics that occupied reviews in the West), or of the clash of generations (which dominated the Soviet critiques of the film). Instead, Moskvina sees what both Western and Soviet reviewers missed: That beyond its critical attitude toward current Russian reality, Pichul's film is set in the "realm of passions."

What Moskvina, one of the most polemic and independent young critics from St. Petersburg, implies here is, in fact, a "depoliticized" view of a film that in the Russia of 1988 was viewed almost exclusively as a social and political statement. Challenging "politically correct" critical standards of *perestroika* as "too obvious not to be boring," Moskvina offers an existentialist, rather than a formalist, interpretation of the picture. We should note that her argument remains within the boundaries of the same tradition against which she subliminally rebels: the tradition of relating art to life, for it is the life force she discusses most in this review. Once more, a close examination of film techniques and aesthetics, as well as a discussion of *Little Vera*'s cinematic context, is absent.

Part of the appeal of Moskvina's piece is her ability to come up with the stylistic precision that does justice to Pichul's "ground-zero" film. In fact, the "tremendous energy" and "savage freshness" on the screen that fascinate the critic apply fully to her review. This is definitely film criticism tuned into a high-voltage power line of enthusiasm.

# CHAPTER VIII

# The Days of Eclipse

A young doctor, Dmitry Malyanov, comes to an unnamed provincial town in Central Asia to work on his dissertation. Everything prevents him from working: unbearable heat, strange people, mysterious omens, alien intervention. Everything is a sign for something else. But what?

*The Days of Eclipse* (*Dni zatmeniya*). Directed by Alexander Sokurov; screenplay by Yuri Arabov, Arcady Strugatsky, Boris Strugatsky, and Pyotr Kadochnikov; based upon a novel *A Billion Years Before the End of the World* by Arcady and Boris Strugatsky; cinematography by Sergei Yurizditsky; production design by Elena Amshinskaya; music by Yuri Khanin. Cast: Alexei Ananishnov, Eskander Umarov, Irina Sokolova, and Vladimir Zamansky. Color, 140 min. Lenfilm Studios production, 1988.

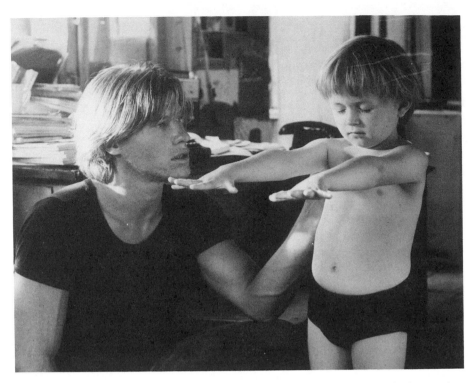

8. A prepubescent angel visits the hero of *The Days of Eclipse* (1988), directed by Alexander Sokurov, heir apparent to Andrei Tarkovsky and the last auteur of the Soviet screen. (Photo: Kinocenter and Sovexportfilm.)

# Out of bounds

*Victor Bozhovich*

This is a strange film, mysterious beyond all limits. I watch it again and again, wandering inside it as if through a labyrinth of ruins. I stumble and freeze, embarrassed and stunned. I am unable to reduce my impressions to one denominator.

Yet the images remain in front of my eyes as if printed on my mind: a dry heat, with its light-absorbing colors; half-ruined mud and straw houses that look like the remains of an earthquake; strange faces; figures, sitting motionless or moving in agony. And over this, there is the atmosphere of disaster, of a psychological coma, of moral stupefaction. The houses are comfortless and strewn with belongings. People seem to be camping out, as if ready to take off for someplace else.

The world on the screen is strangely distorted and dreadfully real, as if in a delirium from which you wish to, but cannot, break away.

Although the film is based on the science-fiction novel by Arcady and Boris Strugatsky, it appears far from any science-fiction element. Any but one: the artistic vision of director Alexander Sokurov, who looks at our earthly life as if from another dimension, through some extraterrestrial's eyes. Nonetheless, such a vision does not alienate us from the screen, but makes us feel what the children feel, lost in the vast, burnt, devastated, and profaned land. The tragic puzzle created by an artist? Or was it life itself that invented it?

# The days of eclipse

*Maya Turovskaya*

This film fascinates some, disappoints others, and baffles the rest. I belong to the first group, not because I admire pretentious truisms on film, but because Alexander Sokurov knows how to develop meaning through an audiovisual structure, and this structure, like music, gives one freedom for a variety of perceptions and interpretations.

The story of a young doctor, isolated in remote Asia while surviving a crisis, relies on a considerably simple social and personal foundation. No one around here lives his or her own natural life: Some are exiles, others assigned to the area by authorities, but all are one way or another transplanted into an alien ethnocultural and ecological environment.

Seen through cinematographer Sergei Yurizditsky's magnificent camera, the yellow mirage of the heat, flooding the screen as if it were fusing space and time, means more than a hot climate: It creates the temporal and spatial dimensions of the picture, its "chronotope" (Bakhtin). On the one hand, the ancient land of the East decays, its signs of degeneration reflected on the people's faces. On the other hand, this land devours the newcomers and initiates their civilization into its own antiquity. The space stretches and warps the time.

I have never seen more powerful images of a landscape obstructed by the emblems of our time. The monumental concrete red star, erected by some ambitious official and eroded by sand, resembles a vestige of a past era, an ancient sphinx for future generations. This ephemeral star, as well as the bust of an unrecognizable leader, evokes the remains of some failed conquest. Entrenched there, in the monotony of the plain and dusty life of a "regional center," one experiences a fusion of times, cultures, and lifestyles. To me, this is what the film represents; others, perhaps, will see in it something else.

The complicated biographies of the "displaced persons" lead us to the relatively recent stratum of our history, in which the Crimean Tartars [exiled by Stalin], for instance, could have been adopted into the family of likewise-exiled Volga Germans. The present, however, is not only interwoven with the past, but opens up to the cosmos, such as in the appearance of the "star boy" in the doctor's house.

**112**

The dialogue between cultures is assimilated into the film's discourse almost without symbolism and fashionable twists. The shot of an ancient woman performing a centuries-old ritual, with classical music emanating from a loudspeaker, as she stands on the deformed concrete slab of an unfinished construction that has become a ruin before having been completed, provides a molecule of meaning to the film. Through its intricate composition, this film, like all Sokurov films, speaks about the important, and shows the touch of a master's hand.

# The world as a mirror for the other world

*Mikhail Yampolsky*

The difficulty of Alexander Sokurov's cinema lies largely in the *multi-worldness* of his films. If in traditional cinema we meet relatively a clear determinism of action caused by reasons within the narrative, in Sokurov's world, the reasons that affect the action in one layer are often hidden in another layer of the discourse. The world we know turns into a mirror for the other world.

Sokurov is one of our few directors who senses the existence of some higher spheres that have been pushed by us beyond the threshold of sensitivity and are now forgotten. These are the spheres where human fate is determined. The mentality of Sokurov's heroes is always limited; they can never comprehend reality as a whole. His heroes' fate depends on more complex and inexplicable reasons than man's will.

Every new picture adds another dimension to the director's universe. The grotesque narrative in *Mournful Unconcern* (1983/1987) was determined by *Heartbreak House*, the George Bernard Shaw play upon which the film was based, and also by the reality of a newsreel, edited into the film. But the causal relations were still mysterious, mystical, and vague.

Sokurov's next feature, *The Days of Eclipse* (1988), reaches out for the extreme intensity of a multiworld universe. The film's structure is built upon the interaction between hermetic and independent universes. The world of Russian culture, personified by the leading character, a young doctor, and Russian soldiers scattered in the background, mysteriously encounters the East. Orthodoxy (the soldiers are portrayed as paradoxical successors of old orthodox missionaries) neighbors with Islam. Life is mystically interlaced with death. Illness penetrates the world of health. The ephemeral instantaneousness of the present is caught up in eternity. The closet world of clinics, which resemble lockups, is impounded in a boundless space. The town where the action takes place looks like a shaky phantom amid deserted mountains: At one point, it reveals its toy nature and at the end simply vanishes.

The most powerful element of this multiworld universe is the universe itself, the cycles to which we are unknowingly submitted. The main event in the film is an eclipse that the characters hardly sense or experience, but

**114**

which explains much in the picture's message. An eclipse traditionally symbolizes the triumph of dark forces over light; it is the sign of the end, a decay of the cosmic cycle. In Buddhism and Islam, an eclipse is associated with a disease of a light source and with death; it is often represented as the cosmic serpent devouring the sun.

Disintegration of both time and causal relations is clearly connected with the symbol of the eclipse. This universal drama is exposed in advance; it penetrates the life of the leading character by mysterious and unintelligible omens. Every now and again, strange animals show up in the doctor's house, for no apparent reason. By mail, he receives a gigantic lobster, frozen in jelly (a hint as to his own case). Then his sister appears out of nowhere with a live hare in a shopping bag. Finally, a huge python sneaks into his room, supposedly an escapee from the neighbors. These animals symbolize constellations: cancer (lobster), hare, and serpent. A serpent directly relates to the idea of a cycle, revival and death, the symbol of the eclipse. It also belongs to the realm of shadows. A cancer is linked to the shadows of the dead and is considered the moon animal, as is a hare.

Thus, the heavenly signs descend onto the earthly world, predicting future events. They explain the cyclic reiteration of time in the film, although they remain a puzzle to the doctor, a last surviving healer of the world, who once was closely tied to astrology. A mythical healer, he had known how to cure people, magically drawing comparisons of their lives to the life of the cosmos. Today's doctor has lost all codes from the oracles: He cannot help anybody, including himself.

The universal scale in *The Days of Eclipse* substantiates Sokurov's perspective. What seems weird, fantastic, and excessive to both the characters and the audience may in fact be the key to existence in Sokurov's world, the core to those causal relations that are placed vertically (between the lines) instead of horizontally (in line).

Ultimately, the segmentation of the life strands in this world reminds us of the tragic egotism of our mentality, and its inevitable separation from the universe – a separation that after many neglectful years of childish optimism we are about to experience as a drama.

# A billion years before the end of cinema

*Tatyana Moskvina*

The Strugatsky brothers have responded rather calmly to the obvious fact that only the names of the main characters have remained unchanged in Alexander Sokurov's *The Days Of Eclipse* (1988), an adaptation of their novel *A Billion Years Before the End of the World*. I understand the sagacious calm of those who have discovered the law of "The Homeostatic Universe."

Moreover, I believe in this law; that is why the director's comment from an interview: "I've never worked as freely as I do now [under *glasnost*]," fills me with joy for both him and the ever-increasing number of free people in all areas of endeavor. But it also fills me with suspicion: Had there not been Oppression, there would have been no discovery, according to the very same law, which is essentially a very Russian one.

It is probably better to return to the novel, not for comparison, but for an examination of it as the director's source of inspiration. It is an enigmatic source, for the lucid, intelligent, logical, entertaining, and witty novel of the Strugatskys and the film *The Days of Eclipse* are not on a par. If you categorize the Strugatskys' books as "B-literature," then you must consider that category to be the noblest of them all. Its moral overview is unshakable. It is a kingdom of sheer mind games and imagination that never delve into – or, more precisely, never find intriguing explanations for – the abyss.

The fantastical adventures of Malyanov, the novel's main character, and his friends are inspired by intellectual pursuits. But the "Homeostatic Universe" does not care for these pursuits; it cares only for the existing balance of power. The Oppression begins, taking the oddest of forms, from common flu, a fire, packages of gourmet delights, and good-looking girls appearing out of thin air to KGB agents implicating an innocent scientist in murder and an ordinary extraterrestrial – anything, as long as it entertains and distracts a person from the intellectual work that threatens the Universal Balance.

It is not by accident that the very idea of the Oppression of the intellect came to our authors in the 1970s. Nor is the minor-key tone of the novel's ending chosen by accident: Everyone has given up, unable to withstand

**116**

the Oppression; only Vecherovsky, a friend of the hero, plans to go far away, to the Asian Pamir mountains, to save himself.

The Strugatskys have turned their sorrow into clever fiction. When Sokurov read their novel, it reminded him, as he confessed in the same interview, of the city of his childhood: "somewhere in the subconscious, it evoked memories of that special world, where people of various ethnic origins lived but where there existed a total cultural vacuum capable of driving even the most unassuming person to desperation." For that very city, the film crew set out.

I think many filmgoers will relate well to this film, and for one reason only: It is not a typical Soviet movie, that "cinema without cinema" that Mikhail Yampolsky blasted in his excellent essay.* The critic warned our film makers: "Film is not only character, plot and conflict transferred onto celluloid but it is also a dance of light, space, sound, face and body on the screen." All these elements can be found in *The Days of Eclipse*, but somehow this "cinema *with* cinema" does not satisfy.

I can well imagine what other journalists will write about *The Days of Eclipse*: "A complex philosophical film has been released that addresses the difficult problems of our complicated lives. This is wonderful, as cinema must be varied." I do not know what those who so stubbornly perpetuate the flaccid contradiction of "complex intellectual" and "simple mass" cultures would do without Sokurov. In today's Russia, Sokurov's films are the last to possess the hallmarks of "complex cinema." Of course, it would be preferable to have more *film auteur*. Then the directors' tendency of reading intellectual tomes would not inflict such fatal tedium on the viewer. Yet today, to protect the lone director who bravely bares his subconscious from insults, many avoid the words "boredom" or "boring" in their critique, although these words usually characterize quite precisely the natural reaction of a living organism to a heavily philosophical film.

The "complexity" of *The Days of Eclipse*, however, derives from a rather simple operation: Having left a few traces of the Oppression (an unexpected package, the intrusion of outsiders, the suicide of the neighbor), the director pulled out the novel's logical pin, leaving its plot disjointed. If, for example, you took out the key words from the phrase "Mikhail S. Gorbachev meets support and understanding from the Americans and President George Bush," you would get: "Mikhail S. faces support from the Bush," a phrase more refined and mysterious, even mystical and "Kafkaesque." Rejection of common logic can only be fruitful when it is substituted by another logic, an artistic logic. It must be true either for the narrative, or for the characters, or for the time and space of the film. It is hard to say this about Sokurov's work.

*The Day of Eclipse* is laden with a series of allusions and symbols that

* See this collection. – Eds.

are supposed to make Sokurov's East (the action is set in some Central Asian Soviet state) more than just an alien location chosen for its exotic flavor. Children here eat pins that x-rays do not detect; a bulb-eyed lizard, nicknamed Joseph, trails the hero; into a room slithers the snake that tempted Eve. These qualifications are mainly verbal and belong to literature rather than to film: Had Malyanov not called the lizard by name (Joseph is hardly an arbitrary name for a predatory reptile – to the Soviets this name automatically conjures up Stalin), or had he not specified that a snake like this seduced the first earthly woman, such oddities would mean nothing but exoticism. By themselves a lizard and a circus python have no real symbolic significance.

Sokurov's East is not at all a multilayered metaphor, as is suggested elsewhere. The director whips up a thick international soup by mixing Turkmenian, Armenian, Azerbaidjani, and Buryat tongues, which resemble the conventional "gur-gur," a meaningless vocal combination used by extras to create the sound of a crowd. Creating his East, Sokurov employed quantity rather than skill and quality. There are a myriad of images, archetypes, and miniscenes inserted into the film instead of a singular image that would have concentrated the full flavor of the East and penetrated the memory forever.

Apparently, the main character and I share a disdain for this environment. Remember, the director spoke of a cultural vacuum, a terrifying world, capable of driving one to desperation. Yet he chose as its hero a man at peace with his surroundings, who ignores its strangeness. Malyanov reacts calmly, which is to say he literally does not react to the awkwardness. It matters little to him where he lives; the most important thing is to complete his work, which is simple – he pounds on a typewriter, the trademark of "an intellectual." This is as convincing as the blinking lights and corridors of scientific machines that are favored in many educational documentaries. In every spare moment, Malyanov hurls himself onto the keyboard and types up a storm. He readily verbalizes the purpose of his work: He has observed that in Baptist and Adventist families, the rate of illness is five times less than in ordinary (atheist? Muslim?) households. To his neighbor, Snegovoi, he specifies the subject of his work: "Juvenile Hypertension in the Families of Pagans." Although it is not clear why Russian Orthodox believers or Protestants are not as lucky, Malyanov's thesis is strikingly original. It turns out that belief in Jesus Christ is beneficial to your health.

If that uninspired pragmatic banality were truly the message of the film, then its level of philosophical sophistication could be confidently declared nil. Apparently, it is not Malyanov's occupation and work that concern the director enraptured by his protagonist. The main thing is that he is a Russian Soviet young man, somewhat stocky, but with a well-developed physique. He sports bleached hair that falls over his face and the distracted half-smile of a youngster who does not know what he wants. Judging by the somersault Malyanov does from the window sill during the eclipse, he would look great on a soccer field or playing ball on the beach. With a typewriter, he is less carefree.

Malyanov's (Alexei Ananishnov) face is like that of an old and solid acquaintance; a face like that looked at us from propaganda posters such as "Glory to Labor," or "The Happiness of Each Is the Concern of All." This face leaves no doubt as to its Slavic origins, but has not a shadow of spirituality. Therefore, when Malyanov turns on the radio to Brezhnev's speech at a Komsomol Congress, it does not appear ironic. He is that very Soviet youth, "dedicated to work" and "overcoming obstacles," the welfare of whom the unforgettable beetle-browed leader claimed to have ensured.

The director obviously thinks that the viewer is still not quite ready for a "cinematic" film, and for more punch, he adds as many verbal comments as possible. Twice Malyanov is told that he is handsome, by his sister and the cherub to whom he replies self-deprecatingly, "And you're observant." His friend Vecherovsky (Eskander Umarov) confirms that "Malyanov has a mark on his forehead." Again, the hero does not deny this but adds that Snegovoi, who committed suicide, also had one. As the viewer only manages to glimpse Snegovoi (Vladimir Zamansky) in the morgue (I detected no such mark), its origin remains a mystery. To me, Vecherovsky's face of a young Tartar prince seemed more significant than that of either Malyanov or Snegovoi. There is also a minor character, Snegovoi's chauffeur, who very well could have had the mark. In response to his employer's question, "And why all this?" he bursts forth with a tirade in Latin.

All these "signs," however, are unlikely to be so craftless and occasional. There is evidently a wisp if not of philosophy then of some point of view. Its interpretation is your choice. Pick one: (1) the hero crossed the boundary while rejecting reality; or (2) he is being punished for the crime of his work; or (3) he is just a nice guy surrounded by a deformed and savage world. But juxtaposing the hero with the life around him does suggest some conclusion. In art, from Sophocles to the Strugatsky brothers, there has been one rule: The hero, violating that which is variously named (circle, order, balance, "Homeostatic Universe," the will of the Gods) undergoes extreme retribution, and, if he enters combat, he most probably dies. The Malyanov of *The Days of Eclipse* sees no battle, but nevertheless is all of a sudden a victor. In the end, he looks with his absentminded half-smile upon the town, which disappears like a mirage. How, with no struggle whatsoever, did he overcome the snake, the lizard, the Russian mission, the visual propaganda and the ethnic nightmare? The director believes so strongly in his hero that he does not feel the need to substantiate anything. Malyanov is portrayed as a positively wonderful person, the town as a horrible apparition. Therefore the town must disappear.

In the advertisement for the movie, Sokurov is called "a fierce revolutionary of film form." By this reasoning, Sokurov's work must be considered alongside that of Tarkovsky, Fassbinder, Buñuel, Antonioni, Resnais, and so on. One need not put him in such an awkward spot: There is not anything in his film that cannot be found elsewhere in world cinema. Assimilating the innovations of others is a natural and indispensable stage, but it is hardly revolution of form. The overt borrowing and imitation, beginning with the title (God bless Antonioni's *L'Eclisse* [1962]), do not bother me at all. The search for lost or unknown ways of thinking or speaking is the healthy desire to rejuvenate culture, to work out its fluid, broad, constant dialogue with any tradition or style. In this general process, Sokurov occupies an indisputable place, but. . . .

Some time ago, critic Alexander Timofeevsky saw in Sokurov's previous film, *Mournful Unconcern* (1983/1987), nothing but the pushing and groundless self-assertion of the director. Then it seemed to me that this shrewd critic was too harsh. Russian film auteur, which is a poor child on thin legs, having just discovered Freud, does not deserve a judgment based on the sense of proportion and conformity. Besides, the biographies of almost all renowned directors prove that one must film a great deal before finding what one is looking for. It is rare when the first or second film happens to be significant – true even among the key film makers.

But today, having watched Sokurov's new movie, made without any oppression, in absolute freedom, I believe that this director imitates rather than authoritatively represents the authorship in film.

# Editors' commentary

Alexander Sokurov's films offer no middle ground for Russian critics. He is a director's director, an auteur's auteur. Clearly influenced by Andrei Tarkovsky, Sokurov has become for the Russia of the 1980s and 1990s what Tarkovsky was for the Russia of the 1960s and 1970s: a prophet, a spiritual healer, a confessor – someone other and more than just a film maker. Sokurov has never made an effort to compromise his artistic vision – not to Soviet ideological cliches, not to the demands of agitated *glasnost*, not to today's changing realities of a market-driven Russian cinema.

This is why the coverage of *The Days of Eclipse* (1988), Sokurov's most accomplished feature of *perestroika* – three short critical exclamations exalting the film, the fourth mercilessly smashing it to smithereens – is not only the broadest but also the most controversial in our collection. Clashing are not simply reviews of a single work, but whole different approaches to film making, indicative of the late-Soviet culture and other world cultures as well.

Unlike the critical duel over *Repentance* (1984), these reviewers' disputes cannot be reduced to the generation gap. If Bozhovich and Turovskaya, who praise the film, belong to the 1960s generation that produced and nurtured the prophetic attitude in art, Yampolsky, a Sokurov supporter so enthusiastic that the film maker dedicated a film to him, and Moskvina, the film's sneering offender, belong to the same younger group of the 1980s. The conflict, therefore, is between two opposing aesthetic perspectives: *auteurist* and *populist*.

The three positive votes are impressed by Sokurov's ability to present a cinematic world that is a mystery wrapped in an enigma. Bozhovich freezes in awe before the film's labyrinth of images. Turovskaya is impressed by the visual play of the dialogue between cultures. And Yampolsky, who builds his thorough review around the "multiworldness" of Sokurov's film, suggests the nonclassical, modernist dimensions of the "vertical" rather than "horizontal" structure. Significantly, none of the three would question the very direction that Sokurov comes from: For them, cinema equals film art, every work of which must be the most personal and intimate reflection of its creator's inner world.

121

When questioned (and not only by Tatyana Moskvina, but also by the new realities of Russian and world culture), the labyrinth of profound images could become a disjointed medley of banalities, a dialogue of cultures, a meaningless vocal combination used by extras to create the sound of a crowd, and the vertical symbolic structure, a boring and pretentious heap of pseudo-philosophical faux revelations.

Moskvina writes with sheer pleasure and cunning wit (humor being, one should note, almost totally absent in Sokurov's as well as in Tarkovsky's films). Moskvina implies that film auteur was healthy for Soviet culture, as film makers confronted the totalitarian "us" with their courageously individualist "I's," the shapeless single-mindedness of one cultural language with a variety of personal styles. Without oppression and with a bohemian distrust to entertainment, Sokurov, being the last true Soviet auteur, became, according to Moskvina, a real double for his character, who supposedly resists some mysterious forces that we never see and, we suspect, do not even exist.

But then again, isn't it what Don Quixote, the archetypal auteur, used to do when he fought against windmills?

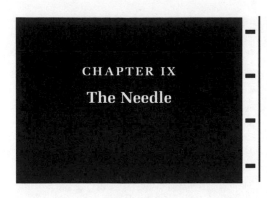

# CHAPTER IX

# The Needle

A young man, Moro, returns to his home town only to find his ex-girlfriend, Dina, becoming a drug addict and himself becoming involved in the bizarre life of the city's underworld. Attempting to save Dina, Moro takes her away to the Aral Sea, turned into a desert by the time they arrive. There Dina seems cured, but back in town everything starts anew. Almost desperate, Moro decides to fight the drug dealers when one of them stabs him in a deserted park.

*The Needle* (*Igla*). Directed by Rashid Nugmanov; written by Alexander Baranov and Bakhyt Kilibaev; cinematography by Murat Nugmanov; production design by Murat Mussin; music by Victor Tsoi. Cast: Victor Tsoi, Marina Smirnova, Pyotr Mamonov, and Alexander Bashyrov. Color, 82 min. Kazakhfilm Studios production, 1988.

9. Emptiness is reflected in the shades of Moro (played by the late rock star Victor Tsoi) in *The Needle* (1988), Rashid Nugmanov's funky meditation on drugs and romance that heralded the Kazakh New Wave. (Photo: Kinocenter and Sovexportfilm.)

# A dandy of the postpunk period or "Goodbye, America, oh..."

*Marina Drozdova*

Goodbye, America, oh,
The land I've never been to.
Your faded blue jeans are
    too tight for me now,
We were taught to love your
    forbidden fruits for so long...

The lyrics from a rock 'n' roll hit song by Nautilus Pompilius sound almost mystical: Being incidental indeed, as any hit lyrics are, they grasp one generation's complex and intricate sensations. Going through adolescence, which life officially grants us for illusions, this generation wore blue jeans (until they were worn out or altered into shorts), secretly read banned literature, studied the Beatles instead of the Bible, and listened to The Voice of America from Washington, D.C., instead of Good Morning, Moscow. California was somewhere out there, where the flower generation's petals had fallen already, but here we had something blooming and flourishing. Despite "Brezhnevism" and "stagnation," life went on, parallel to reality. All potentially disloyal elements were taken under tight control in time for the 1980 Moscow Olympic Games. That was just about time to say goodbye to Elton John's yellow brick road. "Goodbye, America, oh," was our response to Elton John and romanticism of our own unreal life that forked away from "Good Night, Kids" and "The Time," two official Moscow TV programs. Boris Grebenshchikov, the leader of the legendary Aquarium, sang:

Soon this century ends, a marvelous age,
I wonder, if you're sleeping or not?
There's a party today where there's a shelter for us,
But they're hardly waiting for us ...

Bless the generation that lived on the sharp edge between romantic hopelessness and hopeless romanticism.

*The Needle* (1988) comes out of the atmosphere of a long goodbye to

**125**

that romanticism, making the tone of the picture slightly sentimental. The tone supports the melodramatic layer of the narrative, although it is a rather faint blueprint of the traditional melodrama pattern. More than any generic structure, the narrative plunges into the space of the film, an aquariumlike, translucent ambiance. English speakers would describe this narrative as "present continuous"; nothing is "past perfect" here. The tense defines the action, the rhythm, and the characters, and melodrama provides the outward trajectory to the characters' motion. This melodrama unfolds loosely and lazily, consonant to the somnambulistic rhythms of its participants, including the seemingly efficient and dandyish lead, Moro. Played by a legendary rocker, Victor Tsoi, Moro is a dandy of the postpunk period and a knight without fear and reproach.

A brief digression is needed here to distinguish the postpunk styles, here and "there" (the West). Unlike the hippie movement, which followed nothing but natural law, the punks obeyed the rules of the tough game they invented, a game that used the specific sign language of Gothic horror and "black" humor. If the punk culture played according to defined rules, the postpunk culture admits no rules at all; it plays in anything it can find. Our domestic hippies could not help overacting a bit: Clearly, the natural laws of the Berkeley campus and of Moscow's communal flats are quite different. The Soviet punk movement had a chance to emerge much later than that in the West, only when the general situation here had shifted to the left. The postpunk style, on the contrary, did not have any trouble finding a comfortable spot in the minds of this generation. "The philosophy of the image" had come to replace "natural philosophy."

Dandyism, having been a patrician privilege in the past, sprouted in the masses. In *tusovka* (a youth gathering), everyone is a dandy. *The Needle*'s hero fits perfectly into this category.

On an ambiguously reasoned return to his home town, Moro attempts to take Dina, his sweetheart (Marina Smirnova), "off the needle." The story of their affair is the only story in the film that is told in the past perfect tense. Love is gone; only mutual gratitude still remains. Like the romance before, Moro's noble attempt fails.

Arthur, the doctor who put and keeps Dina on the needle, is played by Pyotr Mamonov, the leader of the rock group Zvuki Mu (The Sound of Mu). A virtuoso clerk of Evil who zealously maintains his villainous image, he comes straight from traditional melodrama. So does Dina, a victim who looks like maquillage without a face, paint without a canvas.

But while traditional melodrama is a gold mine of emotions, emotions in *The Needle* slip away. They leak out of the romance and out of all Moro's other relationships, whether it is with his debtor, Spartak, or the doctor who has corrupted Dina. Emotions run, run, run, just like the March Hare in *Alice in Wonderland*, in all directions simultaneously. What remains are shadows of words and ghosts of emotions, quite in tone with the chilly postpunk playfulness, which here has a face of tired eccentricity. Victor Tsoi, slashed by the razor blades of his oriental eyes, looks into the slack space, where everybody has become exhausted by everything. At the same time, our hero seems to be always a step, a frame, a tone ahead of the action. In the finale, fatally stabbed, he does not bleed to death in a lonely night alley, but departs, leaving behind all those "postsweethearts," "postpartners," "postenemies." But where is he heading? To that America where he will never be? (And even if that America exists, is it its geographical reality that attracts us or something else?)

Another dandy is Spartak, brilliantly played by Alexander Bashyrov. How can the social status of this character be determined? Adding a note of "soc-art" to the postpunk feast of *The Needle*, Spartak (a thespian with an assortment of masks himself) masterfully mocks Soviet social and ideological cliches. He plays the game that Moro – a superman, a knight, a poet of himself – has become bored with awhile ago. Spartak is quite far from dull prose himself, but if Moro is a poet, Spartak is a gagman.

We now know where the postpunk dandy comes from in a social sense. Culturally, he originates from the rock 'n' roll lyrics of the past decade – mostly, the lyrics from our "new wave": Kino, DDT, Brigade S, and Nautilus Pompilius. Those angry young men wanted to "break all the walls in the world with their percussions," and those walls were made of people "tied together by chain, tied together by aim, saluting the Chief even when kissing" (Nautilus Pompilius). But is not this anger (charged positively, no doubt) yet another attitude of dandyism, fancy or timely? Anger in *The Needle* is left on the margins of the narrative, perhaps in the city where Moro came from. Moro's game is more esoteric. In this story, he plays a "knight"; who knows what role he will pick next, after he has raised himself up from the blood on that night alley. In any case, that will be another story.

The crowd was swallowing the rock 'n' roll lyrics in the stifling air of underground and concerts (now legalized) and in the smoky kitchens of communal flats. As the images drowned in the youth mass consciousness, they turned into "cult" automatically. All the personal and spiritual values went to the wind, vanished in the heat of reciprocal joy, and only cult silhouettes remained – so convenient for typecasting and shuffling. Most of our last new wave lyrics were intended to become cult. So were some of the images of *The Needle*. That is why the film could be viewed as a kind of comic strip that would like to be considered existential. It is as if Albert Camus's *Stranger* were enacted in forms organic for a different age, retold by means of another cultural language. Although the plots have nothing in common, the characters – both strangers and outcasts – coincide. Camus's manifesto of existentialism alienated the reader, arousing only indifference as one turned the last page. The somnambulistic characters of *The Needle* provoke a similar reaction. All of them are strangers to one another, and the only reason they get involved in a melodrama is that only in melodrama can their ways cross.

Those who fall for analogies in film history recall Godard's *Au bout du souffle* (*Breathless* [1959]). Both Godard's and Camus's characters "accidentally" murdered some incidental people. The lack of Dostoyevskian emotions accentuated the degree of their alienation in the world. Victor Tsoi's character in *The Needle* could not be farther from being a murderer; he is a knight, but indeed an "accidental" one. His inner self is left outside the outline of the character, a stranger to himself. The psychological pattern is the same, only instead of the beach (as in Camus) or the water-colored Place de la Concorde (as in Godard), here we have the arid, fractured Aral Sea and a heap of fallen leaves in the zoo of a god-forsaken provincial town.

In the end, all the inhabitants of this world remain with their backs to one another. No one has deviated from a self-given trajectory. The hero is gone. The party ("Goodbye, America, oh") is over. This moment holds for the characters of *The Needle* like a freeze-frame. So does the "aquarium" space of the picture. Having lost all oxygen, it survives only on an artificial life-support system.

To me, this artificiality drowns the movie. The unfinished game with genre results in dramaturgical uncertainty. If played deftly, this game would be elegant, intelligent, and aesthetically satisfying, but it calls for serious professionalism in addition to true talent. The latter is unquestionable in the case of the director Rashid Nugmanov. As for professionalism, let us attribute a certain shortage of it to the director's young age.

# Editors' commentary

When *The Needle* appeared in 1988, Rashid Nugmanov was perhaps *the* spokesperson for his generation, first in the Soviet Union to use universal culture language to express itself. He was also a founding father of a new movement in Kazakh cinema, "Kazakh New Wave," which, as Marina Drozdova accurately assesses, had more in common with Jean-Luc Godard or Albert Camus than Dostoyevsky. *The Needle* became for the new movement what *Au bout de souffle* (1959) was for its French namesake.

A student of Sergei Solovyev, Nugmanov ventured an experiment similar to that his teacher launched in *Assa* one year earlier. Stronger than anything, he desired a film structure in which *the how* would always dominate *the what*, the language would conquer the substance. In search for new eclecticism, Nugmanov dumped in one pot mannerisms and cliches, stereotypes and archetypes, from Commedia dell'Arte to early Soviet rock 'n' roll, from Godard to Bruce Lee, just as he did with actual languages on the soundtrack, in which Russian, Kazakh, German, Italian, and English create that audio "area rug" Solovyev was dreaming about when making *Assa*. In the heat of *perestroika*, when the democratization of culture had just begun, such pluralism of expressions was more than healthy for a "cinema without cinema" overwhelmed by the subject matter and largely formless.

*The Needle*'s cosmopolitan speech was accentuated by the fact that it was made in Russian in Alma-Ata by a Kazakh who did not speak Kazakh and starred a Soviet–Korean from Leningrad. Understandably, in Marina Drozdova's keen review, the topic of the film's ethnic origin does not seem to be worth discussing. Instead, Drozdova, a young journalist, screenwriter, and socialite from Moscow, takes a loving but critical look at Nugmanov's film from the *inside* of her generation, which also happens to be the hero's and the film maker's generation.

Though Drozdova discusses the genre stereotypes and stylistic peculiarities of *The Needle*, she is clearly more involved in the existential aspects of the life depicted on the screen as she explains how it was possible for a young generation to survive "on the sharp edge between a romantic hopelessness and hopeless romanticism." The critic seems to be unable

**129**

(or unwilling) to concentrate on "decoding" the text – an operation that a text such as *The Needle* suggests. Moreover, her *what*, remarkably, does not contradict the formalist ambitions of the film's *how*. This is because Drozdova accurately places *The Needle* in the context of youth subculture. Being *about* that culture, Nugmanov's film was also a *part* of it – a film dandy, dressed up just like its characters, a statement that belonged to art as much as to the way of life.

# CHAPTER X
# Taxi Blues

Shlykov, a right-wing nationalist Moscow cab driver, tracks down an alcoholic Jewish saxophone player, Lyosha, who has failed to pay his fare one evening. Opposites attract and Shlykov's cruel master–slave treatment of Lyosha turns into a strange kind of friendship and, finally, jealousy as Lyosha becomes an internationally renowned jazz musician, planning to move to New York. In the course of the film's story, the viewer is zoomed, dragged, and yanked through a nightmarish world of lowlife and crime that would hardly have appeared on preglasnost screens.

*Taxi Blues* (*Taxi-blues*). Directed by Pavel Loungin; screenplay by Pavel Loungin; cinematography by Denis Evstigneev; production design by Vadim Yurkevich; music by Vyacheslav Chekasin. Cast: Pyotr Mamonov, Pyotr Zaichenko, Vladimir Kashpur, and Natalia Kolyakanova. Color, 111 min. Ask-Eurofilm, Lenfilm Studios (USSR)–MK-2 Producion (France), 1990.

10. The penniless, alcoholic – and Jewish – saxophonist Lyosha (Pyotr
Mamonov) challenges all that the antisemitic Russian nationalist cabbie Shylkov
(Pyotr Zaitchenko) stands for in *Taxi Blues* (1990), Pavel Loungin's award-
winning French–Russian variation on Mozart and Salieri, set during the twilight
of communism. (Photo: Kinocenter and Sovexportfilm.)

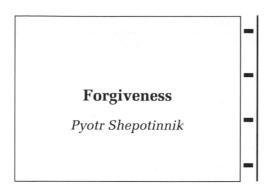

# Forgiveness

*Pyotr Shepotinnik*

For the first time in the history of Soviet film, vignettes, decorated with the fancy Kremlin garlands and depicting the dismal Soviet capital, are labeled with the trademark of a French producer, Marin Karmitz.

Attention to both the East and the West does not tear director Pavel Loungin's *Taxi Blues* (1990) apart. On the contrary, the pompous grandeur of the Stalinist architecture serves as a setting for the wild bohemian slickness that, as acted out by Pyotr Mamonov, appeals to the West. Mamonov, the lead of the postpunk rock group Zvuki Mu (The Sound of Mu), is an *enfant terrible* of the Soviet pop culture. Loungin took his garish public image and polished it by giving his character, the alcoholic saxophonist Lyosha, a 1960s background.

If Lyosha is acceptably Westernized, his opponent, Shlykov, a taxi driver whom Lyosha stiffed for 70 rubles (which would be peanuts today, a year later), is all too Soviet. Hung over, he drinks a typically Soviet "half-and-half": eau-de-cologne diluted with water. His world is stuffed with Soviet trivia: newspapers with the smiling portraits of Lenin serving as wallpaper; tons of garbage mixed with revolutionary posters; cheerful industry reports heard on the radio; and endless, endless lines for vodka. As a generically Soviet character, Shlykov has but one obsession: to teach others how to live. It seems that Loungin could not help falling into the same trap: In trying to balance the social details with psychological nuances, he became hopelessly didactic. Thus, intended as a psychological study, *Taxi Blues* turned into an ideological pamphlet, and this, to me, is its main flaw.

Thrown against each other by a twist of fate, Shlykov and Lyosha gradually become inseparable. Hostaged by the cabbie until he pays back the debt, Lyosha takes a definitive (although not easily definable) place in Shlykov's life. What we have here are two ultimate types of the Soviet citizens: a loyal, hung-over proletarian and a disillusioned, drunk intellectual. Both hate each other. Neither can live without the other.

The two types appeared earlier in Vadim Abdrashitov's 1980 *Fox Hunt*; brought together by chance, they were struck by their mutual discovery and misunderstanding. For Abdrashitov, however, the issue was deeper

**133**

than social discrepancy. From an ideological premise, the movie grew into a philosophical discourse on the tragic impossibility to penetrate the other's life and self, on the dramatic alienation of people who live in the "most democratic" society. What in Abdrashitov's film was a knot of painful contradictions has become, in *Taxi Blues*, a carefully calculated model, glamorously furnished, but always available for easy denotation.

Shlykov, played by an outstanding actor, Pyotr Zaitchenko, is the main nerve of the picture. Like a half-awakened volcano, he erupts unmeasured portions of despair, pity, compassion, and disgust toward Lyosha's lost soul. But he is acting alone, for his opponent, as written and directed by Loungin and played by Mamonov, is an ideological scheme, not a human being. The film makers try to hide the calculation of the character behind the quasi-documentary lyrical digressions into jazz. But the virtuoso sax performance, provided for the movie by a brilliant musician, Vyacheslav Chekasin, makes Lyosha's success look almost immoral, and his pseudo-Mozartian ease rather cynical.

It is not money Shlykov wants from Lyosha, nor is he trying to prove a point. He has been, rather, wounded by his fare's arrogance; what he really wants is for Lyosha to ask his forgiveness. This is the only moment when the dramatic truth overcomes the schematic pattern: The need to forgive and to be forgiven flashes through and lights up the narrative. Shlykov, no matter how good or bad, dumb or intelligent he is, deserves the right to be asked for absolution, not only by Lyosha but by life itself.

Now that the lights in the theater are on and the movie, cheered internationally, is back in the can, a few words instead of an epilogue are in order. Pavel Loungin, just like his hero–jazzman, has settled in Paris and made a new movie, *Luna-Park* (1992). It was shown in Cannes and the director has reportedly signed an American contract. As for *Taxi Blues'* other star, Pyotr Zaitchenko, he lives on the outskirts of Volgograd in a prefab. A telephone was recently – and finally – installed in his apartment. He is flat broke; he cannot even get to Moscow to audition. He thinks he has been forgotten; the Western faxes with congratulations or invitations to festivals vanish somewhere in the Volga.

So maybe we should all ask him to forgive us.

# Taxi fares, blues fans, and film viewers

*Sergei Lavrentiev*

Two circumstances make *Taxi Blues* (1990) a cinematic event.

First is the Jewish question. Mentioned only in passing, it colors with new light the whole story of the love–hate relationship between an ethnic-Russian cab driver and a Jewish saxophone player. Notably, the picture was made before the Jewish question became marketable and director Pavel Loungin had himself exhausted it in his next feature, *Luna-Park* (1992). In *Taxi Blues*, there is no carrying on, no panting, no hysteria about the problem, only subtle and precise indications of it. When the cabby asks the musician, "Are you Jewish?" the question arouses a variable scale of emotions in the audience and does it better than any didactic argument.

The second circumstance that makes *Taxi Blues* an event is the skill with which the film makers combined a typically Russian story with Western dynamics and pace. As a result, we have a "Soviet film of international standards," which our film makers have been dreaming of since the beginning of the end of the Soviet Union.

It is well known far beyond our national borders that Russian directors are attached to verbose "literariness" on the screen and have little faith in visual expression. Loungin's film is quite different. The Soviets' hidden emotional and open social dramas are discussed in *Taxi Blues* in a language comprehensible to people everywhere on this planet.

Many in our country claim that *Taxi Blues* is not a Soviet but a French film. This is true if one agrees that Soviet film is hopelessly provincial. According to popular belief, it was interesting to the world only when it was locked in itself. As soon as the "iron curtain" fell and our cinema found itself in an international cultural context, interest began to decline. Our film makers rushed to "the West."

The number of films made in 1990 was double that for 1989. The world of cinema saw the birth of "a new Hong Kong," building up quantity at the expense of quality. It is not bad that our "independent film" is aspiring to achieve the level of third-rate American movies. In fact, it is quite commendable, as it attests to an objective estimation of our ability. What is really alarming is that even this level turns out to be unattainable.

The lack of imagination and money in the film industry makes stunts

**135**

look ludicrous. Fights are sloppy, for our actors have as little training as our directors have sense of rhythm. The numbers of topless actresses can never transcend into eroticism. And so on. Although this kind of production can count on some success at the local market, it would be totally absurd to assume its ability to conquer the world.

Loungin's combination of the Russian theme, good American rhythm, and French elegance creates a wondrous image of a mysterious country. Everything is out of limits here; people are obsessive and odd, but this country is still a part of the civilized, Christian world.

Remarkably, *Taxi Blues* depicts Moscow mud, Moscow slums, Moscow backyards with the same feeling that Americans use to depict Harlem's skid rows, or Italians the streets of Naples. Old Stalinist critics pigeonholed this approach as "washing dirty laundry in public." However, it would make more sense to regard this style as an attempt to align our coarse canvases with other fabrics of the Old and New Worlds.

All these speculations are for the film's foreign audiences. Clearly, our people loved it simply because, unlike the majority of our films, it is well done.

We are still confused about our own attitude toward commercial cinema and film auteur. We blame the former for the lack of truthfulness and the latter for the lack of popular success. Repeating tirelessly that "a film must be a work of art," we concentrate on "art" and neglect what it looks like.

Watching an Indian melodrama dubbed into Russian in Ukraine, I do not mind that it is out of synch. But when Yuri Mamin's style bumbles through *Sideburns* (1990), I feel that the director, who is warning us against the dangers of Russian national socialism, does not care about the professional flaws in his work. Why, he is making an art film! He is speaking of serious problems!

Most of the domestic success of *Taxi Blues* is owed to young people, the regulars of video clubs. In those stuffy, stuffed rooms, on small fuzzy TV screens, our teenagers see films that may not always be of high artistic value, but that are always technically impeccable. Viewing *Taxi Blues* in a theater, they immediately recognize a film that speaks a language whose basics they already knew.

This part of the audience responds to the outer circle of the narrative, to the swift turns and twists of the plot, and there is nothing wrong with that.

The intellectual members of the audience, who number fewer, can ponder quite different matters. They see, for example, the collision of the main characters not only as a projection of Russian–Jewish love–hatred (and since the film has appeared in the last year of the USSR, Soviet–Western love–hatred), but also as a Russian attempt to reinterpret the traditional American macho myth.

The conflicts, familiar to us from Westerns and gangster films, turn out to be quite feasible in our wondrous Motherland. All that is needed is to replace noble cowboys and fearless mobsters with a cross but kind Russian cabby and a weird but kind Jewish jazzman.

As to the most sophisticated viewers, they may reflect on the homoerotic subtext of the plot. The film gives quite a few grounds, however vague, for such an interpretation. There is also a strange, rationally inexplicable attraction of a proletarian to a bohemian on top of a strange, rationally inexplicable Russian–Jewish attraction–repulsion and a strange, rationally inexplicable fascination of the backward but potentially powerful Soviet Union with the prosperous but somewhat vulnerable West.

In a word, Loungin has managed to do what very few had done in the Soviet cinema before him: a "Napoleon-pastry" film whose layers appeal to all kinds of audiences.

How did it happen? Was it the efforts of the French editors? Or maybe it was incredible directorial power, suddenly invested in a former screenwriter? Both assumptions are fair, given the film's strikingly timely appearance on the screens of the perishing empire.

Not unlike Soviet life before the country's disintegration, *Taxi Blues* is charged with a premonition of changes soon to come. It is seen in the ambiguities of the leads' relationship and the omissions and stylistic incongruities. It is not accidental that at the 1989 Cannes film festival, which presented today's world film culture as a fistfight of neo-academism against neo-barbarism, *Taxi Blues* represented the barbaric tendency. It represented and won, receiving the Best Directing Award.

In the Soviet Union, the film's success was not as spectacular. But the empire was still alive. I believe that later, after the present tempestuous period in Russia is over, film and social historians will understand us better because they have seen Pavel Loungin's film.

# Editors' commentary

Once again (and for the last time in our collection), critical standpoints collide, this time over a film that signaled new directions for Soviet cinema and bridged *glasnost* with the present, posteverything period.

Pyotr Shepotinnik takes a traditionalist stance when he considers *Taxi Blues* (1990) too simplistic to be a work of art. All of his commentary grows from the perspective that has championed works by such directors as Andrei Tarkovsky as "art" and thus worthy of attention, while detesting those who fail to meet the visionary criteria for a "director's cinema." In Shepotinnik's view, *Taxi Blues* suffers from both its status as a coproduction, torn between East and West, and its ideological didacticism.

However, the conventional criteria of auteur theory, apparently, do not fully apply to the new cinema, as seen by writer/director Pavel Loungin, who in one of his American interviews said that he considers himself an "antiauteur" who works in a postauteur culture. Otherwise, had he not run out of his critical instruments, Shepotinnik, perhaps, would not have had to conclude with lamentations on the off-screen matters.

Sergei Lavrentiev, on the other hand, takes a much more open-minded "populist" view of the film, not unlike that of Tatyana Moskvina's view of *The Days of Eclipse* (1988). Lavrentiev's critique exemplifies the stand of a number of younger critics (here represented also by Moskvina, Timofeevsky, and Drozdova) who appreciate the impact of pop culture on high art and who "read" films into the context of that culture in much the way that Pauline Kael (sardonic opponent of the auteur theory) used to discuss American films as outgrowths of trends and currents within the culture.

Aside from praising Loungin's social conscience for introducing the painful subject of the "Jewish question" to general audiences, Lavrentiev applauds Loungin's effort to cross serious director's cinema and pop entertainment by structuring the narrative with a Hollywood pace and dynamism. What the critic is reflecting here is a customary feeling in Russian intellectuals that they want not only entertainment but *well made* (even if superficial) entertainment.

Both reviews were written later than most in this collection, after the

138

end of the Soviet Union in 1991, looking back at one of its last significant films. With the knowledge of what had happened in Russia, Lavrentiev concludes: "Not unlike Soviet life before the country's disintegration, *Taxi Blues* is charged with a premonition of changes soon to come." Loungin's film, which has done exceptionally well around the world, truly stands at the crossroads: not only between high art and pop culture, but also between *perestroika* and free-market, chaos-driven, post-Communist Russia. As a material for film critics, it presents, along with our two final reviews, the changing requirements, values, criteria, and techniques that Russian film criticism will have to adopt in the years to come.

# Conclusion

# Beyond glasnost

*Marina Drozdova*

## Death of the word

Before speculating on the end of Soviet cinema, we should kiss goodbye anything "Soviet." The word has lost its meaning in all things, not just in geographic imperialism and political status. From the map, the word has traveled straight into history textbooks.

What then shall we call the movies made on the territory of the former Soviet Union? It is much easier to call the territory "Russia" than the films made on it "Russian," because the national aesthetic tradition is long gone. Nothing but myth is left of it. The problem is being solved rather trivially today: Bad films are known as "cooperative" films, mediocre films as "glasnost" films, and good ones as simply "films."

## Absence of location

One could not find a location for shooting in today's Russia: The country has just been exhausted. All that is left on display perches on the edge of emergency: St. Petersburg, a few forests, a couple of fields and rivers. But it would be next to impossible to clean them up enough to create pleasant locations. They are suitable for nothing but condemnation and criticism, with which both viewers and film makers, even the most daring in the recent past, have become bored.

Although everything old has crumbled, there is neither time nor money to build anew. The film necessities – nails and sets, paints and makeup, bulbs and lights, fabrics and costumes, let alone camera and sound equipment – have performed a universal vanishing act. It is as if, in a flashback, we have gone back to the Lumière period: There is an idea of the cinema, but there is almost nothing to realize it with. Consequently, the good film makers do not get involved in predictably unrealizable projects, whereas the bad film makers reduce interiors on the screen to a cheap used furniture store on the verge of going out of business.

This crisis of form parallels the crisis of content. Along with the death of other old Soviet myths, the "Bright Future" has moved from the future

**143**

to overseas, specifically to the United States. The transition from a communal to an individualistic mythology is painful. Formerly "Soviet" film is facing a future similar to that of the former empire: survival by imitating the West. To a society used to seeing itself as a main course, the idea of becoming dessert is new and frightening.

## Death of the former hero

Since the system collapsed, the cinema of the CIS has eagerly engaged in recasting. Directly or indirectly, openly or secretly, the majority of film makers borrow from film models already established.

The politics of borrowing has revealed a curious incongruity: Just as Russia exhausted its own reality, the civilized world has done the same with its own normality. Neo-conservatism has evoked preoccupation with the Other, who imitates the norm but does not comply with it. The Other, a mutant, has become a favorite character both for commercial and for art film in the West. Unlike the Nietzschean "Superman," the "Post-man" refuses to dominate the world. As a product of computerized mentality and ecological disaster, he is too involved with himself.

In Europe, after the totalitarian madness of the war and postwar regimes, the notion of a mutant has emerged organically from the idea of a socially perverted self in which an ideological myth has replaced reality. In Western and Eastern European cinemas, the process was scrupulously examined by such masters as R. W. Fassbinder, Istvan Szabo, and Andrzej Wajda, whereas for the cinema of the former Soviet empire, this level of analysis was hardly accessible, even during *glasnost*.

In the West of the late 1980s, a new version of the mutant appeared on the screen: a transsexual or sexless one. In a strange equation, "transsexual" in him/her meant "transsocial," and "sexless" meant "nonsocietal." By that time, pop culture was already led by two exemplar "children of the tube" (television or chemical?), Madonna and Michael Jackson.

By 1992, the mutant finally arrived on the formerly "Soviet" screen, denoting the death of the former hero. Most spectacularly, it is manifested in director Oleg Kovalov's film, *The Gardens of Scorpion* (1992).

Kovalov decided not to bother scouting nonexistent locations; his film is made up of fragments from Soviet movies shot between 1926 and 1964, its skeleton extracted from *The Case of Corporal Kochetkov*, which was made in 1955 by an order of the Defense Ministry of the USSR. In that banal, propagandistic story, typical of the early Cold War years, a soldier falls in love with a girl; she turns out to be a spy and he reveals the conspiracy.

A thorough reediting totally changed the "biology" of the original from a vulgar witch-hunt story to a lyrical love story. By looping the shots and making them longer, Kovalov turned the girl's evil look into a tender one and the soldier's mindless marching into a tormented Hamletlike pacing. Montage and remontage created a gigantic system of mirrors that reflected the mythological hero, clipped out of the phantasmagorical Stalinist reality. A postmodern Dr. Frankenstein, the director recreated a human being out of a mythological monster that imitated humanness, but was in fact deprived of it.

If Kovalov's film is made of "other" material, so is *Kicks* (1992) by Sergei Livnev. This time, the material is imported not from the past, but from the West. *Kicks* is our most European "Soviet" film. Nothing "domestic" is left in this story about a concert manager who replaces his protege, a drug-addicted rock 'n' roll star, with her double. Not unlike an android that copies a human being, the stand-in copies the looks and mannerisms of her idol, and life in *Kicks* is but an imitation of life.

In the recent past, it seemed as if audiences wanted to see movies about their own lives, but their lives dressed and furnished according to the alien, Western standard. Perestroika made "overseas" look accessible. Some even thought that by saving and economizing, "our" life could be arranged "their" way. But as the free market spread, the euphoria shrunk. The dollar looks good all around, but the salary keeps coming in rubles. There are practically no Soviet movies playing in the country, although people now want them. At last people want to see themselves.

## The end of the ruble

Not only is our cinema uninformed about how to manage money behind the camera, but it is ignorant about how to manage money on the screen. The scripts are bursting with racketeers, gangsters, and ordinary citizens who want to get rich by any (often dishonest) means. But because the ruble means less than nothing today, it is unclear what the stakes are in these screen wars. And it is unclear to everybody: the characters, the actors, the writers, and the film makers.

Money as a motif and dramatic cause had been badly devalued by the Russian and particularly Soviet art. Money had become a somewhat shameful and meaningless "capitalist" atavism. Today, as the screen is suddenly filled with new Russian businessmen, a new syndrome has developed – financial impotence. As soon as a safe or a wallet fills the frame, the film makers' creativity comes to a deadlock. Only one film over the past five years has treated the subject wittily: Stolen money was sewn into a dead body. Regrettably, inflation devalued the gimmick between the film's production and its release.

Fiction can never catch up with life. Here is the story the Moscow film world was laughing about: The boss of the central animation studio has sold the rights to the pictures of Yuri Norstein, a world-famous animator whose *Tale of Tales* (1978) was once named the best animated film of all time. With that money, the executive bought sugar to distribute among the studio employees at a time when sugar had vanished from the stores. Not only did Norstein, who was not a studio employee, not receive any royalty, he did not get any sugar either.

## The light at the end of the tunnel

Despite all the problems, there must be a light at the end of the tunnel. What is left in Russia to be filmed? Pure spirit. And recently, we had quite a few examples of successful screen adaptations of pure spirit – the human spirit, the spirit of culture, the spirit of history. These films include Alexei Balabanov's *Happy Days* (1991), based on Samuel Beckett's works; Irina Yevteyeva's *A Horse, a Violin and a Bit Nervously* (1992), a film essay inspired by the verse of a futurist poet, Vladimir Mayakovsky; *The Desert* (1991) by Mikhail Katz, a reinterpretation of the biblical legend; and several others.

These films and their makers work in peace with themselves, ignoring fleeting changes in film and in life. They are as self-sufficient as the ideal metric measure, made of gold and stored somewhere in Paris, completely useless. Instead, plastic rulers are being used. And this is the way it is.

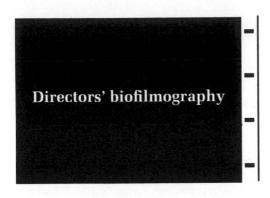

# Directors' biofilmography

The following provides biographical and filmographical information about the directors of the films, discussed in Part Two. The entries are arranged in alphabetical order.

**TENGIZ ABULADZE** is one of the originators of the "Georgian School" of film. Born in 1924 in Tbilisi, he was educated at the Tbilisi Theatre Institute (1943–6) and at the National State Film Institute (VGIK) from which he graduated in 1953. He wrote or co-wrote most of his films.

> *Magdana's Lurdzha* (1955, codirected with Revaz Chkheidze; Grand Prix for the Best Short Film at the Cannes Film Festival, 1956)
>
> *Strange Children* (*Strannye deti*, 1958)
>
> *Me, My Grandmother, Iliko and Illarion* (*Ya, babushka, Iliko i Illarion*; 1963)
>
> *Supplication [The Prayer]* (*Mol'ba*; 1968, based on the poem by Vazha Pshavela; Grand Prix at the San-Remo Festival, 1979)
>
> *A Necklace For My Beloved* (*Ozherelye dlya moei lyubimoi*; 1973)
>
> *The Wishing Tree* (*Drevo zhelaniya*; 1977; Award at the Carlovy Vary Film Festival, 1978; "David Donatello" Award in Venice)
>
> *Repentance* (*Pokayanie*; 1984; Special Jury Award at the Cannes Film Festival, 1987)

**ALEXANDER ASKOLDOV** received his Masters degree in Philology from the Literary Institute in Moscow. He worked as an editor in Goskino (Soviet Ministry of Cinema), and then graduated the Higher Courses of Film Directors and Screenwriters, a two-year graduate program in film production, affiliated with Mosfilm Studios. *Commissar*, his first and only feature film, followed in 1967. After banning *Commissar*, the People's Court of Babushkinsky District of Moscow declared Askoldov "professionally unfit." He was fired from the Maxim Gorky Film Studio, expelled from the Communist Party, and consequently prosecuted for "voluntary unemployment." Since then Askoldov acted as an executive director of the Rossiya concert hall in Moscow. After *Commissar* premiered in July 1987 at the Fifteenth International Moscow Film Festival, it received international fame and multiple awards, including the Silver Bear and The International Critics' Award at the Berlin Film Festival (1988).

**PAVEL LOUNGIN** was born in Moscow in 1949. After studying structural linguistics at Moscow University, he became a professional screenwriter, author of many unproduced and eleven produced scripts. *Taxi Blues*, his first feature as director, shot in 1990, won him Best Director award at Cannes. His latest film, *Luna-Park* (1992), played at many international festivals, including Cannes, Toronto, and others.

**RASHID NUGMANOV** was born in 1954. While a student at VGIK, he made his debut with *Ya-kh-ha* (1986), a short semidocumentary about the Leningrad underground scene. He graduated in 1987 with *The Art of Being Submissive* (*Iskusstvo byt' smirnym*), which he wrote and directed. Since *The Needle* (1988), his only completed feature is *The Wild East* (*Dikii vostok*, 1993).

**VASILY PICHUL**'s (born in 1961) VGIK thesis film was *Whose Are You, Old Folks?* (*Vy chyo, starichyo?*, 1983). *Little Vera* (1988), his next feature, brought him international success and notoriety at home. The film was screened and awarded at many festivals, including Chicago (the Golden Hugo Award) and Montreal. Since then, Pichul has completed two features, *The Nights Are Dark In the Town of Sochi* (*V gorode Sochi temnye nochi*, 1989) and *Idiot's Dreams* (*Mechty idiota*, 1993).

**JURIS PODNIEKS** was born in Latvia in 1950. He received a degree in cinematography from VGIK in 1975 and made his name as a cameraman at the Riga Film Studio before directing his first documentary. Since *Is It Easy To Be Young?* (1987), Podnieks has completed a 5-hour documentary series *Us* (*My*, 1990) about perestroika for the BBC, *The Cross Way* (*Krestny Put*, 1991), and *The End of the Empire* (Konets Imperii, 1992). During the work on his next project, Juris Podnieks died in a drowning accident in 1992. He also directed the following documentaries:

> *Mount, Boys!* (*Po konyam, mal'chiki*, 1979)
>
> *Yurmala* (1981)
>
> *Constellation of the Archers* (*Sozvezdiye Strelkov*, 1982)
>
> *Yaunkemery* (1982)
>
> *24 Summer Hours* (*24 letnikh chasa*, 1983)
>
> *Commander* (*Kommandir*, 1984)
>
> *Sisyphus Rolls a Stone* (*Katit Sizyph kamen'*, 1986)

**ALEXANDER PROSHKIN** received his degree in Drama Directing from the Leningrad State Institute of Theater, Music and Film in 1961, at the age of 21. *The*

*Cold Summer of '53* (1987) marked his shift from television to feature film making. His latest feature is *To See Paris and Die* (Uvidet' Parizh i umeret', 1992). Other films include:

> *The Strategy of Risk (Strategiya riska*, TV film, 1978)
>
> *Inspector Gool* (TV film, 1980, based upon a play *An Inspector Calls* by J. B. Priestley)
>
> *Dangerous Age (Opasnyi vozrast*, TV film, 1981)
>
> *Mikhailo Lomonosov* (TV miniseries, nine episodes, 1986)

**ELDAR RYAZANOV** (b. 1927) belongs to the older generation of Soviet film makers. After graduating from VGIK, he began making documentaries and then switched to comedies. He since has become a patriarch of Russian comedy and won multiple State Awards of the USSR. Besides directing and co-writing his films, he writes prose, plays, and poetry.

> *Carnival Night (Karnaval'naya noch*, 1956; Honorary Diploma at the 1957 Edinburgh Film Festival; Award at the I Moscow Film Festival, 1958)
>
> *A Girl Without an Address (Devushka bez adresa*, 1957)
>
> *A Man From Nowhere (Chelovek niotkuda*, 1961)
>
> *The Hussar Ballad (Gusarskaya ballada*, 1962; Jury Diploma at the Third Comedy Film Festival in Vienna, 1963)
>
> *Give Me the Book of Complaints (Daite zhalobnuyu knigu*, 1964)
>
> *Beware Of the Automobile (Beregis' avtomobilya*, 1966; Honorary Diplomas at the 1966 Edinburgh Film Festival, the 1966 International Film Festival in Sydney, and the 1967 International Film Festival in Melbourne)
>
> *Zigzag of Fortune (Zigzag udachi*, 1968)
>
> *Grey-haired Bandits (Stariki razboiniki*, 1972)
>
> *The Incredible Adventures of the Italians in Russia (Neveroyatnye prikliucheniya italiantsev v Rossii*, 1974; Soviet–Italian)
>
> *The Irony of Fate (Ironiya sud'by, ili s legkim parom*, 1977)
>
> *An Office Romance (Sluzhebnyi roman*, 1978)
>
> *Garage (Garazh*, 1979)
>
> *Put In a Word For a Poor Hussar . . . (O bednom gusare zamolvite slovo. . .*, 1980, TV film)
>
> *Train Station For Two (Vokzal dlya dvoikh*, 1982)

*The Ruthless Romance (Zhestokii romans*, 1984; Golden Peacock at the 10th International Film Festival in New Delhi, 1985)

*A Forgotten Tune for the Flute (Zabytaya melodiya dlya fleity*, 1987)

*Dear Elena Sergeyevna (Dorogaya Elena Sergeevna*, 1988)

*The Promised Sky (Nebesa obetovannye*, 1991)

*The Prophecy (Predskazaniye*, 1993)

**ALEXANDER SOKUROV**, born in 1951, holds a degree in history from the State University of the City of Gorky and in film making from VGIK. After working for the television station in Gorky, he came to St. Petersburg where he soon became the most controversial, avant-garde, and stigmatized Soviet filmmaker of the late 1970s–1980s.

*Man's Lonely Voice (Odinokii golos cheloveka*, 1978, restored in 1987, a thesis project; Bronze Leopard at the 1987 International Film Festival in Locarno)

*The Demoted (Razzhalovannyi*, 1980, short)

*Sonata for Viola: Dmitry Shostakovich (Al'tovaya sonata: Dmitri Shostakovich*, 1981/1987, codirected with Semen Aranovich, documentary)

*Composer Shostakovich (Kompozitor Shostakovich*, 1981, documentary).

*The Allies (Soyuzniki*, 1982, documentary)

*And Nothing More (I nichego bol'she*, 1983/1987, documentary)

*Patterns On The Ice (Uzory na l'du*, 1985, documentary)

*Patience. Labor. (Terpeniye. Trud.*, 1985/1987, documentary)

*Mournful Unconcern (Skorbnoye beschuvstviye*, 1983/1987, based upon a play *Heartbreak House* by George Bernard Shaw)

*Elegy (Elegia*, 1985/1986, documentary; FIPRESSI Prize at the 1986 International Film Festival in Tampere)

*The Evening Sacrifice (Zhertva vechernyaya*, 1984/1987, documentary)

*The Empire Style (Ampir*, 1987, short)

*The Moscow Elegy (Moscovskaya Elegia*, 1987, documentary)

*The Days of Eclipse (Dni zatmeniya*, 1988; European Academy Award for the best soundtrack, West Berlin, 1988)

*Maria* (1988, documentary)

*Save and Protect (Spasi i sohrani*, 1989, based upon a novel *Madame Bovary* by Gustav Flaubert; FIPRESSI Prize at the 1989 Montreal International Film Festival)

*The Soviet Elegy* (*Sovetskaya Elegia*, 1989, documentary)

*The Second Circle* (*Krug vtoroi*, 1991)

*Stone* (*Kamen'*, 1992)

Before *Assa* (1987), **SERGEI SOLOVYEV** was best known in the Soviet Union for his adaptations of Russian classics and films about teenagers. He was born in 1944 and accepted to VGIK at 17. At the age of 22, Solovyev wrote a screenplay for a documentary short, *Look at the Face*, which received an award at the Leipzig Documentary Film Festival. Today, he combines his work as a producer and film maker with teaching film production at VGIK and at the Higher Courses of Film Directors and Screenwriters. He also runs a production unit at the former Mosfilm Studios.

*The Proposal* (*Predlozheniye*, 1970, based upon two short stories by Anton Chekhov; in the feature presentation, *Familial Bliss* (*Semeinoye schastye*))

*Yegor Bulychev and Others* (*Yegor Bulychev i drugiye*, 1974, based upon a play by Maxim Gorky)

*Station Master* (*Stantsionnyi smotritel'*, 1972, TV film, based upon a novella by Alexander Pushkin; Grand Prix for Best Television Production at the Venice Film Festival, Euro-Vision Award)

*One Hundred Days After Childhood* (*Sto dnei posle detstva*, 1975; Best Director Award at the Berlin Film Festival, 1976, Grand Prix at the International Youth Film Festival in Belgrade, Silver Medal at the Avellino Film Festival, State Prize of the USSR, 1977)

*Melodies of the White Nights* (*Melodii beloi nochi*, 1977, Soviet–Japanese coproduction)

*Life-Guard* (*Spasatel'*, 1980; Special Award at the Venice Film Festival)

*The Heiress* (*Naslednitsa po pryamoi*, 1982; Gold Medal at the 13th Festival of Children Films in Salerno)

*The Chosen* (*Izbrannye*, 1983, Soviet–Colombian coproduction)

*The Wild Pigeon* (*Chuzhaya belaya i Ryaboi*, 1986; The Jury Grand Prix at the Venice Film Festival)

*Assa* (1987)

*Black Rose Stands for Sorrow, Red Rose Stands for Love* (*Chernaya roza – emblema pechali, krasnaya roza – emblema lyubvi*, 1989)

*The House Under the Starry Sky* (*Dom pod zvezdnym nebom*, 1991)

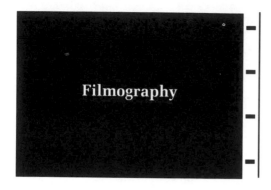

# Filmography

Only the films discussed in the main text, and not the films listed under the "Directors' Biofilmography" are included in this general filmography. The films marked with an asterisk after the English title are reviewed in Part Two of this collection.

**Anemia** (1988). Dir. Vakhtang Kotetishvili

**Arsonists, The** (*Podzhigateli*, 1989). Dir. Alexander Surin

**Ashik Kerib** (1988). Dir. Sergei Paradjanov

**Assa\*** (1987). Dir. Sergei Solovyev

**Au bout du souffle** (***Breathless***, 1959). Dir. Jean-Luc Godard (France)

**Baby Doll** (*Kukolka* 1988). Dir. Isaac Fridbergs

**Ballad of a Soldier** (*Ballada o soldate*, 1959). Dir. Grigori Chukhrai

**Battle for a Fleet** (*Bitva za flot*, 1989). Dirs. Alexei Feoktistov and the Che-payev Group

**Battleship Potemkin** (*Bronenosets Potemkin*, 1925). Dir. Sergei Eisenstein

**Beware of the Automobile** (*Beregis' avtomobilya*, 1966). Dir. Eldar Ryazanov

**Blackmailer, The** (*Shantazhist*, 1988). Dir. Valery Kurykin

**Black Monk, The** (*Chernyi monakh*, 1988). Dir. Ivan Dykhovichny

**Black Rose Stands for Sorrow, Red Rose Stands for Love** (*Chernaya roza – emblema pechali, krasnaya roza – emblema liubvi*, 1989). Dir. Sergei Solovyev

**BOMZH** (1988). Dir. Nikolai Skuibin

**Brick Flag, The** (*Kirpichnyi flag*, 1988). Documentary; dir. Saulius Berzhinis

**Brief Encounters** (*Korotkiye vstrechi*, 1968). Dir. Kira Muratova

**Bright Path, The** (*Svetlyi put'*, 1940). Dir. Grigori Alexandrov

**Burglar, The** (*Vzlomshchik*, 1987). Dir. Valery Ogorodnikov

**Case of Corporal Kochetkov, The** (*Sluchai s efreitorom Kochetkovym*, 1955). Dir. Alexander Razumnyi

**Circus, The** (*Tsirk*, 1936). Dir. Grigori Alexandrov.

**Close to Eden** (*Urga*, 1992). Dir. Nikita Mikhalkov.

**Cloud Paradise** (*Oblako-rai*, 1992). Dir. Nikolai Dostal

**Cold Summer of '53, The\*** (*Kholodnoye leto 53-go*, 1987). Dir. Alexander Proshkin

*Color of Pomegranates, The* (*Tsvet granata*, 1969). Dir. Sergei Paradjanov

*Coming Closer* (*Priblizheniye*, 1991). Dir. Alexander Rekhviashvili

*Commissar** (*Komissar*, 1967). Dir. Alexander Askoldov

*Comrade Chkalov's Crossing of the North Pole* (*Perehod tovarishcha Chkalova cherez Severnyi polius*, 1989). Short; dir. Maxim Pezhemsky

*Confession: The Chronicle of Alienation* (*Ispoved': Kronika otchuzhdeniya*, 1988). Docudrama; dir. Georgi Gavrilov

*Crew, The* (*Ekipazh*, 1980). Dir. Alexander Mitta

*Cruel Male Disease, The* (*Zhestokaya bolezn' muzhchin*, 1987). Short; dirs. Igor Aleinikov and Gleb Aleinikov

*Daddy, Santa Claus Is Dead* (*Papa, umer Ded Moroz*, 1992). Dir. Yevgeny Yufit

*Dark Eyes* (*Ochi chernyie*, 1987). Dir. Nikita Mikhalkov (Italy)

*Daydreams* (*Grezy*, 1988). Short; dir. Yevgeny Kondratyev

*Days of Eclipse, The** (*Dni zatmeniya*, 1988). Dir. Alexander Sokurov

*Dear Elena Sergeyevna* (*Dorogaya Elena Sergeyevna*, 1988). Dir. Eldar Ryazanov.

*Defense's Summing-Up, The* (*Slovo dlya zashchity*, 1976). Dir. Vadim Abdrashitov

*Desert, The* (*Pustynya*, 1991). Dir. Mikhail Katz

*Dissident* (1989). Dir. Valery Zheregi

*Escriva Isaura* (1989). TV miniseries (Brazil)

*Evening Sacrifice, The* (*Zhertva vechernyaya*, 1984, released in 1987). Documentary; dir. Alexander Sokurov

*Fire in the Nature* (*Ogon' v prirode*, 1988). Short; dir. Yevgeny Kondratyev

*First Blood* (1982). Dir. Ted Kotcheff (United States)

*Flights at Night and in Daydreams, The* (*Polyoty vo sne i nayavu*, 1983). Dir. Roman Balayan

*Forgotten Tune for the Flute, A** (*Zabytaya melodiya dlya fleity*, 1987). Dir. Eldar Ryazanov

*Fox Hunt, The* (*Okhota na lis*, 1980). Dir. Vadim Abdrashitov

*Frozen Cherry, The* (*Zimnyaya vishnya*, 1987). Dir. Igor Maslennikov

*Garage, The* (*Garazh*, 1980). Dir. Eldar Ryazanov

*Garden, The* (*Sad*, 1984). Short; dir. Alexander Kaidanovsky

*Gardens of Scorpion, The* (*Sady skorpiona*, 1992). Dir. Oleg Kovalov

*Georgian Chronicle of the 19th Century, The* (*Gruzinskaya khronika XIX veka*, 1979). Dir. Alexander Rekhviashvili

*Guest, The* (*Gost'*, 1988). Short; dir. Alexander Kaidanovsky

*Happy Days* (*Schastlivyie denyochki*, 1991). Dir. Alexei Balabanov

*Harlan County, USA* (1977). Documentary; dir. Barbara Kopple

*Heiress, The* (*Naslednitsa po pryamoi*, 1982). Dir. Sergei Solovyev

*Homunculus, The* (*Gomunkulus*, 1989). Dir. Alexander Karpov

*Horse, a Violin and a Bit Nervously, A* (*Loshad', skripka i nemnozhko nervno*, 1992). Dir. Irina Yevteyeva

*Husband and Daughter of Tamara Alexandrovna, The* (*Muzh i doch' Tamary Alexandrovny*, 1989). Dir. Olga Narutskaya

*I Am Twenty* (*Mne dvadtzat' let*, 1963, released in 1965). Dir. Marlen Khutsiev

*Idiot Am I to Forget . . .* (*Ya zabyl, debil*, 1986). Short; dir. Yevgeny Kondratyev

*Ilyich Square* (*Ploshchad' Ilyicha*), see *I Am Twenty*

*Incident on a Regional Scale, The* (*ChPe raionnogo masshtaba*, 1988). Dir. Sergei Snezhkin

*Intergirl* (*Interdevochka*, 1989). Dir. Pyotr Todorovsky

*Irony of Fate, The* (*Ironiya sud'by, ili s legkim parom*, 1975). Dir. Eldar Ryazanov

*Is It Easy to Be Young?*\* (*Legko li byt' molodym?*, 1986). Documentary; dir. Juris Podnieks

*Is Stalin With Us?* (*Stalin s nami?*, 1989). Documentary; dir. Tofik Shakhverdiev

*It* (*Ono*, 1989). Dir. Sergei Ovcharov

*Kerosene Seller's Wife, The* (*Zhena kerosinshchika* 1989). Dir. Alexander Kaidanovsky

*Kicks* (1992). Dir. Sergei Livnev

*King of Crime, The* (*Vory v zakone* [*Thieves in Law*], 1988). Dir. Yuri Kara

*Kiss, The* (*Potselui*, 1983). Dir. Roman Balayan

*Knights of Heaven, The* (*Rytsari podnebesya*, 1989). Dir. Yevgeny Yufit

*L'Eclisse* (*The Eclipse*, 1962). Dir. Michelangelo Antonioni (Italy–France)

*Left-Hander, The* (*Levsha*, 1988). Dir. Sergei Ovcharov

*Legend of the Suram Fortress, The* (*Legenda o Suramskoi kreposti*, 1984). Dir. Sergei Paradjanov

*Letters from a Dead Man* (*Pis'ma mertvogo cheloveka*, 1987). Dir. Konstantin Lopushansky

*Little Fish In Love* (*Vliublennaya rybka*, 1989). Dir. Abai Karpykov

*Little Vera*\* (*Malen'kaya Vera*, 1988). Dir. Vasily Pichul

*Longest Day, The* (1962). Dirs. Bernhard Wicki and others (United States)

*Long Farewell* (*Dolgiye provody*, 1971). Dir. Kira Muratova

*Lumberjack* (*Lesorub*, 1985). Short; dirs. Yevgeny Yufit, Yevgeny Kondratiev, and Oleg Kotelnikov

*Luna-Park* (1992). Dir. Pavel Loungin (France–Russia)

*Manservant, The [The Servant]* (*Sluga*, 1989). Dir. Vadim Abdrashitov

*Man's Lonely Voice, A* (*Odinokii golos cheloveka*, 1978/1987). Dir. Alexander Sokurov

*Meeting Place Cannot Be Changed, The* (*Mesto vstrechi izmenit' nel'zya*, 1979). TV; dir. Stanislav Govorukhin

*Mirror, The* (*Zerkalo*, 1975). Dir. Andrei Tarkovsky

*Mirror for a Hero, A* (*Zerkalo dlya geroya*, 1988). Dir. Vladimir Khotinenko

*Moscow Does Not Believe in Tears* (*Moskva slezam ne verit*, 1979). Dir. Vladimir Men'shov

*Mournful Unconcern* (*Skorbnoye beschuvstviye*, 1983/1987). Dir. Alexander Sokurov

*Mr. Decorator* (*Gospodin oformitel'*, 1987). Dir. Oleg Teptsov

*My Friend Ivan Lapshin* (*Moi droug Ivan Lapshin*, 1984). Dir. Alexei German

*Name Day, The* (*Den' angela*, 1988). Dirs. Sergei Selyanov and Nikolai Makarov

*Nazar's Last Prayer* (1988). Dir. Levan Tutberidze

*Needle, The** (*Igla*, 1988). Dir. Rashid Nugmanov

*Night of the Living Dead* (1968). Dir. George Romero (United States)

*Nine Days of One Year* (*Devyat' dnei odnogo goda*, 1961). Dir. Mikhail Romm

*Oath, The* (*Klyatva*, 1937). Dir. Alexander Usoltsev

*Office Romance, An* (*Sluzhebnyi roman*, 1978). Dir. Eldar Ryazanov

*Once Upon A Time in the West* (1969). Dir. Sergio Leone (United States–Italy)

*Orderly Werewolves, The* (*Sanitary-oborotni*, 1985). Short; dir. Yevgeny Yufit

*Planet Parade, The* (*Parad planet*, 1984). Dir. Vadim Abdrashitov

*Plumbum or, A Dangerous Game* (*Pliumbum, ili Opasnaya igra*, 1987). Dir. Vadim Abdrashitov

*Post-Political Cinema, The* (*Postpoliticheskoye kino*, 1988). Short; dirs. Igor Aleinikov and Gleb Aleinikov

*Prishvin's Paper Eyes* (*Bumazhnye glaza Prishvina*, 1989). Dir. Valery Ogorodnikov

*Promised Sky, The* (*Nebesa Obetovannye*, 1991) Dir. Eldar Ryazanov.

*Put In a Word For a Poor Hussar . . .* (*O bednom gusare zamolvite şlovo . . .* , 1980). TV; dir. Eldar Ryazanov

*Rambo: First Blood Part II* (1985). Dir. George P. Cosmatos (Unites States)

*Repentance** (*Pokayaniye*, 1984). Dir. Tengiz Abuladze

*Report Form the Land of Love, The* (*Reportazh is strany liubvi*, 1988). Dir. Pyotr Pospelov

*Revolution Square* (*Ploshchad' Revolyutsii*, 1989). Documentary; dir. Alexander Ivankin

*Rock* (*Rok*, 1988). Documentary; dir. Alexei Uchitel

*Roger and Me* (1989). Documentary; dir. Michael Moore

*Rumble Fish* (1983). Dir. Francis Ford Coppola (United States)

*Ruthless Romance, The* (*Zhestokii romans*, 1984). Dir. Eldar Ryazanov

*Seventeen Moments of Spring* (*Semnadzat' mgnovenii vesny*, 1973). TV; dir. Tatyana Lioznova

*Sideburns [Whiskers]* (*Bakenbardy*, 1990). Dir. Yuri Mamin

*Simple Death, The* (*Prostaya smert'*, 1985). Dir. Alexander Kaidanovsky

*Solitary Cruising* (*Odinochnoye plavanye*, 1985). Dir. Mikhail Tumanishvili

*Solovki Regime, The* (*Vlast' solovetskaya*, 1988). Documentary; dir. Marina Goldovskaya

*Somebody Was Here* (*Zdes' kto-to byl*, 1989). Dirs. Igor Aleinikov and Gleb Aleinikov

*Spot, The* (*Pyatno*, 1985). Dir. Alexander Tsabadze

*Spring* (*Vesna*, 1946). Dir. Grigori Alexandrov

*Spring* (*Vesna*, 1987). Short; dir. Yevgeny Yufit

*Star Wars* (1977). Dir. George Lucas (United States)

*Step, The* (*Stupen'*, 1986). Dir. Alexander Rekhviashvili

*Tale of Tales, The* (*Skazka skazok*, 1978). Animation; dir. Yuri Norstein

*Tarzan, The Ape Man* (1932). Dir. W. S. Van Dyke (United States)

*Taxi Blues** (1990). Dir. Pavel Loungin (France–Soviet Union)

*Temptation* (*Soblazn*, 1988). Dir. Vyacheslav Sorokin

*Three, The* (*Troye*, 1988). Dirs. Alexander Baranov and Bakhyt Kilibayev

*Tractor Drivers, The* (*Traktoristy*, 1992). Dirs. Igor Aleinikov and Gleb Aleinikov

*Tractors, The* (*Traktora*, 1987). Short; dirs. Igor Aleinikov and Gleb Aleinikov

*Tragedy in Rock* (*Tragediya v stile rok*, 1988). Dir. Savva Kulish

*Train Has Stopped, The* (*Ostanovilsya poezd*, 1982). Dir. Vadim Abdrashitov

*Train Station for Two, The* (*Vokzal dlya dvoikh*, 1982). Dir. Eldar Ryazanov

*Trash* (1970). Dir. Paul Morissey (United States)

*Trial on the Road* (*Proverka na dorogakh*, 1971/1986). Dir. Alexei German

*Turn, The* (*Povorot*, 1978). Dir. Vadim Abdrashitov

*Twenty Days Without War* (*Dvadtsat' dnei bez voiny*, 1978). Dir. Alexei German

*Twist of Fate, The* (*Peremena uchasti*, 1987). Dir. Kira Muratova

*Visitor to a Museum* (*Posetitel' muzeya*, 1989). Dir. Konstantin Lopushansky

*Volga, Volga* (1938). Dir. Grigori Alexandrov

*Waiting for DeBill* (*V ozhidanii DeBila*, 1991). Dirs. Igor Aleinikov and Gleb Aleinikov

*Way Home, The* (*Put' domoi*, 1983). Dir. Alexander Rekhviashvili

*Wild Pigeon, The* (*Chuzhaya belaya i Ryaboi*, 1986). Dir. Sergei Solovyev

*Wings of Desire* (1988). Dir. Wim Wenders (Germany–France)

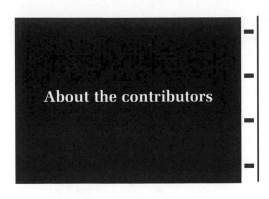

# About the contributors

**IGOR ALEINIKOV** is one of the leaders of the Parallel cinema, an independent avant-garde movement; producer, director and critic; publisher of *Cine Phantom*, the first independent film publication in the Soviet Union.

**LEV ANNINSKY** began his career as a literary, theater, and film critic in the 1950s. He is an author of numerous books and articles on the classical and contemporary Russian culture.

**YURI BOGOMOLOV** is a film critic, author of several books and numerous articles on Soviet film, television, and popular culture. In the late 1980s, he became one of the first professional Soviet columnists for *Sovetskii ekran* and *Iskusstvo kino* film magazines.

**VICTOR BOZHOVICH** is a film and culture critic and historian whose area of expertise spreads from French art of the turn of the century to contemporary Russian film.

**SERGEI DOBROTVORSKY**, at 35, holds a Ph.D. in Cinema Studies in one hand, and the banner of counterculture in another. He is a film critic, sociologist, and producer who helped to launch and led the Parallel cinema movement in Leningrad. He is also a screenwriter whose last produced screenplay, *Nicotine* (1993), was a remake of *Au bout de souffle* (1959).

**MARINA DROZDOVA** is a young freelance journalist, film critic, and an author of several screenplays. Since 1985, she contributes frequently to *Iskusstvo kino, Sovetskii Ekran*, and other film publications.

**LEV KARAKHAN**, who is a deputy editor-in-chief of *Iskusstvo kino*, writes frequently on film industries of the former Soviet republics.

**TATYANA KHLOPLYANKINA**, a VGIK Screenwriting Department graduate, published her first review in 1958. Since then, she wrote several produced screenplays, such as *Ticket to the Movies* (1981) and *Who Is Knocking at My Door?* (1983), and became the Arts Department staff writer for *Literaturnaya Gazeta* (*Literary Ga-*

*zette*), one of the most popular Soviet newspapers where she worked until her untimely decease in 1993.

**ALEXANDER KISELEV**, a young journalist and screenwriter, served on staff of *Sovetskii film*, published in Moscow in several languages, until the magazine closed due to budgetary difficulties. Presently, he works for Arkeion Films, a French–Russian joint venture.

**SERGEI LAVRENTIEV** is a film critic and a curator for *Illusion*, a Moscow art and revival theater house.

**TATYANA MOSKVINA** is a St. Petersburg–based film critic and journalist, whose passion for the movies began in her early teens and made her one of the leading young critical voices in the years of perestroika.

**PYOTR SHEPOTINNIK** is Foreign Film department editor of *Iskusstvo kino* and a host of a popular national television program on film.

**ALEXANDER TIMOFEEVSKY** is a Moscow-based freelancer, considered by many the most influential film critic of the glasnost generation. His articles have appeared in all major Russian publications.

**MIKHAIL TROFIMENKOV**, who turned 19 when Gorbachev announced glasnost, has since become a mouthpiece for the contemporary Russian avant-garde. His articles have appeared in the Russian, Latvian, Swedish, and American periodicals.

**MAYA TUROVSKAYA**, who has led the Soviet cultural elite during the years of Khrushchev's "thaw," remains an active theater, film, and literary critic. Her most recent book, published in English, was *Tarkovsky: Cinema as Poetry*.

**MIKHAIL YAMPOLSKY** is a culture theoretician, semiologist, and champion of Russian film *auteur*. He currently teaches at New York University.

**About the editors**

**MICHAEL BRASHINSKY** teaches film studies at Brooklyn College, The School of Visual Arts and The New School in New York City. Originally from Leningrad, he has written for major Soviet and American film journals and magazines. He is a coauthor of *The Zero Hour: Glasnost and Soviet Cinema in Transition* (with Andrew Horton, Princeton University Press, 1992).

**ANDREW HORTON** is a professor of film and literature at Loyola University in New Orleans and a professional screenwriter. He has written widely on European, American, and East European cinemas. His most recent books are *Comedy/Cinema/Theory* (University of California Press, 1991) and *The Zero Hour: Glasnost and Soviet Cinema in Transition* (with Michael Brashinsky).

# INDEX